Rock Bottom Wisdom

ROCK BOTTOM WISDOM

OR

FROM ROCK BOTTOM TO WISDOM

ACCOUNTS OF MEN AND WOMEN WHO WENT FROM
A SEASON OF DEEP SUFFERING TO A MEANINGFUL LIFE.

HOW THE 'GIFT OF DESPERATION' BROUGHT THEM TO
'A LIFE BEYOND THEIR WILDEST DREAMS'.

YVELINE ARNAUD

REACH
PUBLISHERS

ISBN 978-1-3999-5070-1

Published by Yveline Arnaud using Reach Publishers' services,
P O Box 1384, Wandsbeck, South Africa, 3631

Edited by Gil Harper for Reach Publishers
Cover designed by Reach Publishers
Website: www.reachpublishers.org
E-mail: reach@reachpublish.co.za

YVELINE ARNAUD
sereneline@googlemail.com

Table of Contents

How this Came to Be

A few years ago, I investigated the beliefs of Alcoholics Anonymous (AA) members as my subject of choice for an MSc in Addiction Psychology and Counselling.

I attended open AA meetings[1], spoke to AA members and arranged interviews. I was pleasantly surprised by their initial warm welcome and later by the depth of their answers to my questions.

I kept thinking of those *fellows*, as they call themselves, who had experienced such an amazing transformation. They trusted me with intensely personal matters. Interviewing them was like harvesting jewels.

As the saying goes, "Wisdom is better than rubies; and all the things that may be desired are not to be compared to it."[2]

Those interviews yielded a rich crop of wisdom cultivated by ordinary folks who had found something better than rubies. Even the shyest among them were eager to share what they had acquired as if sharing their treasures multiplied them. As lovers know well, sharing pleasures does multiply them.

There was much to learn from those interview transcripts. They addressed issues people commonly have to face. Everybody endures lows, whether accompanied by anxiety, loneliness, grief or more.

---

[1] Open to non-members

[2] *King James Version* of the Bible (KJV), Proverbs 8:11.

Later, I met a different type of person who displayed a rare peace of mind. I arranged to interview them also and then found they had some commonalities with fellows in recovery. Both these groups of people had emerged from their hardships wiser and happier. They will be met here.

In Part One, AA members share how their lives became meaningful. In Part Two, non-alcoholics tell how they have seemingly stumbled on a life of "abundant joy".

Can wisdom come to us after we hit rock bottom? Can rock bottom be a stepping stone to a new dimension? Can hardships lead to joy?

Now in 2023, living in a world where anxiety dominates our general atmosphere, we might have to examine our lives and straighten out areas that need it. I hope these intimate lessons will help you in that process.

PART ONE

FINDING RECOVERY – AA MEMBERS' ACCOUNTS

Definitions

Alcoholics Anonymous (AA) is defined in the *Webster's College Dictionary*[3] as "an international fellowship of alcoholics whose purpose is to stay sober and help others recover from alcoholism".

It is also the title of AA's main book, affectionately called *The Big Book* by AA members. Its first part contains instructions on how to acquire sobriety. Its second part tells the life stories of some original AA members.

Alcoholism, as defined by the AA, is a chronic physical, mental and spiritual illness, "a progressive illness that can never be cured but which, like some other diseases, can be arrested"[4].

Higher Power (HP) is an expression "left up to the individual to decide how they wish to define it. There are no rules except that this power has to be greater than the individual"[5].

Recovery is "a special term used in AA... to connote the process by which alcoholics become abstinent and undergo the self-help/mutual aid journey to heal the self, relations with others, one's HP and the larger world"[6].

---

[3] Random House Kernerman, K Dictionaries Ltd, 2010.

[4] *44 Questions pamphlet*, 1952, New York: Alcoholics Anonymous World Services, Inc., 1990.

[5] http://alcoholrehab.com/alcohol-rehab/higher-power-in-aa

[6] Borkman T., *The twelve-step recovery model of AA: a voluntary mutual help association*. Recent Developments in Alcohol 18: 9-35, 2008.

The 12-Step Programme is "a program... designed specially to help an individual overcome an addiction... by adherence to 12 tenets emphasizing personal growth and dependence on a higher spiritual being"[7].

Prayer has had various different definitions. A simple one is, "Prayer is, at [its] root, simply paying attention to God"[8].

A sponsor is someone who works with another or others less advanced in AA recovery to help them apply the Steps and the programme to their lives.

---

[7] http:// www.merriam-webster.com/dictionary/12-step

[8] Martin R., The Fulfilment of All Desire, Emmaus Road Publishing, USA, 2006.

Introduction

Amerian psychiatrist M. Scott Peck wrote in *Further Along the Road Less Travelled,* "I believe the greatest positive event of the twentieth century occurred in Akron, Ohio, on June 10, 1935, when Bill W and Dr Bob convened the first AA meeting. It was not only the beginning of the self-help movement and the beginning of the integration of science and spirituality at a grass-root level but also the beginning of the community movement."[9]

As "the greatest positive event" of the last century, it deserves to be taken seriously and should probably not be confined to AA members or members of the other Anonymous groups.

In the same book, Scott Peck suggests, "If you feel you need psychotherapy, but you can't afford it, then one thing you could do is to pretend you're an alcoholic, go to AA and get yourself a sponsor. There are actually some people who do that... [or] pretend you've got an alcoholic relative and go to AlAnon[10] ... Actually, you don't have to pretend. Undoubtedly somewhere in your family you do have an alcoholic relative." (p. 144)

An old friend of mine found that he did not even have to pretend he was an alcoholic to go to AA. He had been suffering from depression for most of his life. Not an addict in the usual sense of the word, he was only

---

[9] Ed. Simon & Schuster, 1993, p. 150.

[10] Fellowship of relatives of alcoholics – their programme is based on the 12-Step programme of *Alcoholics Anonymous* adapted for families.

addicted to "his own way of thinking", as Richard Rohr suggests we all are.[11]

He had spent much time ruminating on negative thoughts. His own way of thinking would pull him down. He unsuccessfully tried Prozac and other antidepressants. Then he considered AA, initially out of curiosity.

Seeing he was well-received as a visitor to an open AA meeting, he returned and became that group's only non-alcoholic regular member. Two years later, he realised his depression had lifted. He had applied to his own life the Steps that were helping AA members to recover from alcohol addiction. Thus, he learned and adopted a way of life that led to his recovery from depression.

Years later, when I saw him again, he was still free from depression. He enjoyed a good recovery, continuing to apply what he had learned during his time in AA.

My friend might be an isolated case; however, Peck recommends attending AA to anyone wanting counselling. He sees hope of recovery in it for those in need.

Addictions of the mind? Can they be treated as other addictions?

According to Rohr's observations, some disorders can be viewed as addictions to thought processes. If so, what would those who are afflicted by anxiety, negative

[11] A Roman Catholic monk, Rohr has authored various books. He leads retreats and lectures internationally. Having attended numerous AA meetings as a visitor, he wrote *Breathing Under Water, Spirituality and the Twelve Steps*, SPCK Publishing, 2018. He believes everyone is an addict in that everyone is addicted to their own way of thinking. Whether or not we accept this theory, the lessons learned by people in the grip of alcoholism who achieve great and contented lives can be applied to non-alcoholics.

thinking or other symptoms of depression have in common with alcoholics?

Alcohol dependence includes all aspects of the person. The *Alcoholics Anonymous* book shows that drinking is the tip of the iceberg of a malady in a physically, mentally, and spiritually sick person. Only treating the physical element is like trying to cut off the top of the iceberg, hoping to get rid of it this way. Yet, the hidden part holds the underlying reasons for the addiction – traumas, pain, depression, and other factors that might elude not only onlookers but also the addict himself. The largest portion of the illness remains underneath and that is where the commonality between alcoholism and other physical, mental, and spiritual sicknesses lies. The difference is in the fact that the alcoholic, as well as the other substance addicts, seeks temporary relief from those painful states that a substance offers. Note that many people who are depressed get addicted to prescription drugs.

Can the programme of recovery offered by AA and other 12-Step fellowships be applied to some mental health problems or disorders not medically classified as addictions?

Much has been written about what keeps people sober in AA, but perhaps more information is needed about what helps alcoholics in AA to acquire the "life beyond [their] wildest dreams" that their programme promises. "The short-term goals are to attain and maintain sobriety. The long-term goals are to live a life of joy and happiness, of purpose and meaning."[12]

That is a tall order, way beyond what people commonly

---

[12] *Alcoholics Anonymous*, 2001, p. XXVI.

aim for in their life. Would AA have discovered, or maybe reframed, in a more acceptable way, some old principles from which others could benefit? Addict or not, who would not want "a life beyond [their] wildest dreams"? The fact is that a journey into the AA programme may yield recovery for whoever is willing to embark on it.

The metamorphosis of the caterpillar into a butterfly illustrates some people's journey. Getting out from the cocoon is apparently a painful process, yet if someone tries to 'help' shorten it by opening up that cocoon with scissors, the butterfly will not be able to fly. It is the effort of pushing out of the chrysalis that brings fluid into the wings, which is necessary to strengthen the wings and complete the butterfly. This is the process of transformation from an immature form to an adult form. Interviews of AA members who have received the 'gift of sobriety' and what is for them a more meaningful life show that their experience is comparable to the caterpillar's. When followed seriously, the AA programme takes individuals from what are often states of depression all the way to lives "of joy and happiness, purpose and meaning". That is why it "has been called the most significant phenomenon in the history of ideas in the twentieth century."[13]

What can people who are not seen (or do not see themselves) as addicts gain from such a program? First, there needs to be a willingness to try it. Prejudices deters many. What in this programme could attract people who are not seen as addicts?

---

[13] Kurtz & Ketcham, *The Spirituality of Imperfection*, Bantam Doubleday Dell, 2002, p. 4.

It might have something to do with reaching the end of one's rope or reaching rock bottom, as happened to my friend Peter when he was in depression. It was then he thought about going to AA.

CHAPTER 1

Anger, Resentment, Depression, and Alcohol

Trying to resist suffering generally worsens it. When a woman in labour resists her contractions, she experiences more pain.

When we fight against pain, the circumstances of our lives generally cause us more suffering. The *Serenity Prayer*[14], routinely prayed in AA meetings, opens with the wise words, "God, grant me the serenity to *accept* the things I cannot change".

Nobody can avoid pain altogether. It is part of life. Lasting anger, resentment or anxiety are some of the negative emotions people try to avoid and sometimes hide, even from themselves. However, seeking the numbing effect of addictive substances as a refuge, inexorably brings worse long-term consequences. That is when those who use alcohol to self-medicate[15] their depressed feelings risk becoming alcoholics.

Anger is a normal human emotion, but it must be expressed safely, or it is dangerous. It is also addictive. Its chemical effect on the brain reward pathway is similar

---

[14] *The Serenity prayer*, "God, grant me the serenity to accept the things I cannot change, the courage to change the things I can and the wisdom to know the difference" was written by the American theologian Reinhold Niebuhr around 1932.

[15] "At least two-thirds of alcohol-dependent individuals entering treatment show evidence of anxiety, sadness, depression and/or manic-like symptoms... self-medication has been proposed as an explanation for alcohol consumption in people with... anxiety and depression." Cornah D., Cheers? *Understanding the Relationship Between Alcohol and Mental Health*, Mental Health Foundation, 2006.

to that of an addictive substance. It causes a surge of adrenaline accompanied by a type of pleasure, but the consequences can range from violence to a host of health problems.

Behind alcohol and other substance addictions, there is usually anger. It may have been "pushed down" (buried). Later, it might come out dangerously, especially when *under the influence*. When buried, anger grows with time, and its accompanying resentment turns to bitterness.

AA members may remember various symptoms of depression from their past. They have perhaps concealed anger and resentment. Hidden or not, resentment is a major reason people become and remain alcoholics. The *Alcoholics Anonymous* book says, "Resentment is the number one offender: it destroys more alcoholics than anything else."[16]

Unresolved resentment poisons those who harbour it and often results in physical illnesses. They may consciously or unconsciously turn against themselves. In extreme cases, people have committed suicide as 'revenge' against those who hurt them. The habit of alcoholism itself is a form of slow suicide.

AA is about breaking the suicidal pattern by building new habits. "What AA provides... is a method for attacking the *habits* that surround alcohol use. AA, in essence, is a giant machine for changing habit loops."[17]

---

[16] Fourth Edition, 2001, p.64.
[17] Duhigg, *The Power of Habits*, Random House, 2013, p.69.

TO DEAL WITH RESENTMENT

In the course of the AA programme, personal resentments are inventoried. The AA book indicates, "in dealing with resentments, we set them on paper."

When Annie did that, it led her to a new, healthy, and liberating solution. Now in her fifties, she had been a *functioning alcoholic* for many years, during which she was able to keep up a professional front.

Behind that front, she was in denial, oblivious to her alcoholism and even to her suicidal ideation. Despite being a danger to herself, she was surprised when she was sectioned in a mental hospital, and she could not understand why her psychiatrist transferred her to the Addiction Treatment Programme of the clinic: she had functioned so well that she had fooled herself into believing she was a normal drinker. She was as much in denial about her alcoholism as about her depression.

Yet, behind her façade, she was obsessed with resentment. She blamed her unhappiness on past traumas – her experience of early abuse, her parents' divorce, and other difficult events she had gone through. She used to ruminate over the many conflicts she remembered.

"If I had an upset during the day, I would relate it to something, like maybe an argument I had had with my dad twenty or thirty years before, and then I would be drinking. My head would never stop and let go of the past."

In AA, she realised that her obsessions over the past had prevented her from living in the present.

"My past was my present... and it was soon to become my future."

Richard Carlson describes what that means for many people. "To break free from unhappiness, you have to bring yourself to the present. You must realize that your past is no longer there – it's over... The truth is that many arguments, painful confrontations, or difficult situations are only difficult because people are busy thinking about the past without realizing they are doing so... filtering their present moments through thoughts of the past...interfering with the present experience of healthy functioning."[18]

To obsessively rehash resentments is a characteristic that addicts and people that are low in mood may have in common. In AA and other Anonymous 12-Step fellowships, people use a vivid illustration for it: pointing to their forehead, they go in circles with their index finger, calling it "the washing machine" as a metaphor for the repeated cycle.

For the first time, Annie was able to identify with other people. It happened during an AA meeting and set her on a path of self-discovery. She agreed to follow the programme "to the best of her ability"[19] which made it possible for her to start changing. She realised that it would be extremely dangerous for her sanity and sobriety to keep blaming others or her past.

The strategy that she adopted for dealing with her resentments can be a good model for whoever feels resentful.

"I know that I have to find forgiveness. No matter what happened and what I may think, blaming is not going to be the answer to any of my problems. So, whereas

---

[18] Carlson R., Stop *Thinking, Start Living*, Element 2003, p. 61.

[19] This is a very comforting saying in AA: nobody is expected to follow the programme perfectly, but members are only expected to do it "to the best of their ability".

before I would have blamed my whole past on how I was, today I accept I am 100% responsible for how I am."

That shift in her pattern of reasoning resulted in a new way of dealing with the temptation to become resentful that might occur in her everyday life.

"Now, I don't have a single thought about the past. *If anything happens, I keep it in the day*."

She learned that no matter what happened and what she might think, *blaming was not going to be the answer to her problems*. Before AA, she could blame her whole past for how she was feeling. Her newly found solution was to accept being completely responsible for how she felt.

Blaming and the ensuing bitterness are known to be at the origin of many physical illnesses as serious as cancer and mental illnesses as extreme as paranoia.

RESENTMENTS IN DEPRESSION

AA members talk openly about the insanity of their condition. When they first enter recovery, they might have been *dual diagnosed*[20]: on top of their alcoholism, they suffered from other mental health problems. As they use the recovery programme and become sober, some people get the added bonus of recovering from a mental condition that had been previously amplified by their addiction.

This was John's case. A distinguished-looking man in his thirties, he had been diagnosed as manic

---

[20] It is common for addicts to be also diagnosed with a mental illness, hence the dual diagnosis. When the addiction is treated, the underlying mental illness might disappear as it did in John's case.

depressive (bipolar). Psychotic depression alternated with manic episodes. It was when he entered the AA 12-Step programme that he realised he had been dual-diagnosed.

"I was at a meeting last night, and it was about step two, '*Came to believe a power greater than ourselves could restore us to sanity*.' Well, I *was* clinically insane when I came into AA. I had an alcoholic bipolar psychosis, and I don't have that anymore. I am no longer insane!"

Describing his past depression, he spoke about the depth of resentment that had accompanied it. It had given him a dark perspective of everyone in general. In AA, he experienced a shift when his opinions of others and handling of relationships dramatically improved.

"I had a terribly negative view of people and their motivations. I thought they were selfish, self-centred at best, and cruel and vindictive at most. That's changed."

He became more unselfish and stopped judging people so negatively. He realised judging and criticising resulted from projecting *his own negative motivations* onto them. That understanding is illustrated by the simple saying, typically told to children, "When you point the finger at someone else, three other fingers are pointed at yourself." So does one's pointed finger in critical judgment of others usually hide a critical and judgemental mind. Recognising it in oneself is a good first step.

At the same time, John was learning that honesty was a fundamental condition for recovery. Many people are critical and judgemental and do not realise that they hurt themselves by keeping such a mindset. The 12-Step programme shows a better way.

John took that better way when he learned to examine his motivations and estimate whether they were ethically right. He accepted the AA requirement of working on himself. Then he was able to see others' good motivations or intentions.

"I certainly think there are people who don't behave in a good way, but that probably the majority of people *want* to be good, even if they aren't. That's actually a very big shift. I think a lot of it is about not being so self-centred and not seeing the world revolving around me, not being so self-focused, and about trying to think about other people and to act in ways that are good."

As he did, he became aware of an old belief he had held dear, which had also spoiled his moods. He had thought that happiness was his due.

"From a mental health kind of perspective, I was not grateful for anything at the end of my drinking... It requires work to be happy – or contented. It's *not* an entitlement. That is definitely a new thing for me!"

To fancy happiness as a due is a common expectation. It automatically leads to disappointment. Because of it, people become rebellious, oblivious to the fact that they are not *owed* happiness. That attitude of entitlement may result in resenting the very fact that they will, at times, meet difficult circumstances. It prevents them from looking at themselves and working on their recovery, which is a good way to get more contentment.

ESCAPIST BEHAVIOURS

Mark, a middle-aged English man, comes from an alcoholic family. He came to realise that, like his relatives who had passed away, he was on a sure path to death.

"As a result of not wanting to die, I wanted to stop drinking... not wanting to die a miserable death because I'd seen it first-hand in the family."

Depression was common among his relatives. In his turn, for years, he found life unmanageable. He was unable to cope with what he called "the pain, the suffering, the finding-it-difficult".

The mental suffering endured in depression is often at the origin of escapist behaviours such as excessive drinking. Mark also tried other ones.

"Anger, shouting, gambling, smoking weed, sexual obsessions, eating and working disorders – they come in many forms of impulsive actions, just to go with the bad and the negative. Our *inner addict* and disease twist our thinking to justify the selfish escapist behaviours. I have self-gratified... I had experiences with LSD when I would look back and it was frightening. I was gripped with fear, cold fear."

For a long time, he had followed the path of untreated alcoholism. It leads to some form of death.

"I just wanted my life to end. There is a choice between life and death... You can choose to carry on drinking and die."

While in AA, he became more aware of the faults in his reasonings. He saw that he had made wrong decisions. However, along with this new awareness, he became more sensitive to other people's character defects. While he perceived people's motivations better, he noticed he tended to slip from discernment to resentment.

"I can sense my own irritation and impatience, and the most frustrating thing is that being able to read people's motivations, I can make a judgement quickly, which I *don't* want to make. I can't help it. I'm hoping that, as I search further, I will remove that...."

He was particularly vulnerable in the area of couple relationships. He learned to deal with his tendency to be resentful when his ex-girlfriend falsely accused him of harassment. He found that unfair but learnt a deep lesson from it.

"I had one romantic relationship in recovery. It was very difficult at the time to feel those intimate emotions and then to separate. It was painful for me. I believed that I'd been wronged, and I wasn't the one in the wrong. She was very vindictive. She went to the police and said that I'd harassed her. She told lies. There was a sense of injustice... I wrestled with righteous anger."

When he accepted to face both his suffering and the situation, the pain slowly died. Presented with a choice, he could have refused to accept what he recognised as a message of truth. But he learned and grew from it.

"Refusing it would create suffering even greater than the pain I was trying to avoid. And *I grew up from sitting with that pain*. I'd never suffered with a broken heart before, but it was an enormous growing-up experience for me because it made me really embrace this programme. It makes you *look at your part only, not the other person's part*...."

He looked at his part in the situation, honestly asking himself what he had done or was doing wrong, and he saw it. He then allowed his pain to lead him toward inner healing *and* more ethical living.

"I wanted to fight back, but the opposite was to look at what happened, 'How did you allow yourself to get into that situation? What were your motivations? Why? Knowing what's happened in this woman's life, how could she? Put yourself in her shoes and just imagine her perception, knowing she's got these insecure emotions! *Not to think* about your own, just to think about her.' And I opened both out – my mind and her own issues."

Though he had first felt revengeful, he started to have compassion for her. From that moment, he understood more about himself and his own true motives.

"I could see her and that we were just entities trying our hardest. It taught me a lot about my nature as a partner and my nature to dominate, to be in control, to be aggressive, not physically, but to be aggressive, which I wouldn't have looked at before."

Looking at his part was the opposite of his usual self-centred attitude, but it is what helped him to accept and take the situation calmly and what taught him so much.

It is a known fact in AA that what you concentrate on will grow like a plant that you feed. That is one of the reasons people are encouraged not to focus on unhelpful thoughts but to focus on positive ones.

A good question to ask is, *"What kind of thought cells do we want to cultivate in the garden of our brain?"* Asking himself an equivalent to that question, Mark considered the unhelpful thoughts he habitually entertained.

"For a long time, I was self-righteous. I had to accept that that's part of me. It's there. 'Face it. It's probably not going to go away, so face it!' Like I've faced these other things. 'See what it is... Where does it come from? What does it eat? Deny it that food and hopefully we won't see it very often. But accept the fact that it's there and it won't go away...' It catches me by surprise sometimes, but not as much as it used to."

Being honest with himself about his wrong motives had a healing effect on him.

Healing is also one of the effects of listening to others who talk honestly, opening up about their weaknesses in AA meetings. Those who listen well will identify similar weaknesses in themselves and learn ways to deal with them. Thus, hearing others describe their faults and bad choices can break through the denial behind which addicts try to hide.

LONELINESS AND POWERLESSNESS

Active alcoholics may have a busy social life, but it is usually a superficial one and they feel lonely inside. As the progressive illness of alcoholism worsens, the social life becomes increasingly restricted, and the feeling of loneliness might lead to depression.

Conversely, depression without substance addiction commonly includes a feeling of loneliness.

Fred, an older man, was a loner. For most of his life, he had been isolated. While in a rehab centre for alcoholism, he was oriented to an AA support group. Soon after he came out of rehab, he went on a prolonged binge. When he emerged from it, he realised that he could not keep sober by himself. He also saw that there was a mental health issue behind his addiction.

"It made me realise that I can't do it by myself... I'd be stark-raving mad."

On top of his loneliness, he admitted he was powerless over certain attitudes that had kept him drinking heavily for a long time.

"I was naturally very lazy, stubborn, arrogant and selfish... and I thought I was morally quite correct! I'd think I knew it all. These are the traits that kept me ill."

Seeing those traits in himself, most likely by hearing people honestly confessing them, was an eye-opener for a man who had always thought he was "morally quite correct". It had a liberating effect on him. He was no longer isolated in his own world, thanks to seeing the similarities between himself and others.

PAIN, INSECURITY AND FEELING ALIENATED

Lily, a woman in her thirties, had grown up in a dysfunctional family. Consequently, she found life difficult, always feeling on the outside of society, not quite belonging.

"Underneath, there is pain. I'm feeling a deep insecurity, spiritually bankrupt, completely alienated. I'm uncomfortable, lost."

This feeling of insecurity is familiar to those who are depressed, whether they are in active addiction or not. Lily could not see a purpose in her life and often wondered about the meaning of existence. Obsessing on those questions used to pull her down.

"What's the point of living? What's the meaning, the purpose? Why be here? What for?"

Famous psychiatrist and Auschwitz survivor Viktor Frankl explored these questions. In his book, *Man's Search for Meaning*[21], he noted that people who had survived the Nazi concentration camps were not the strongest nor the cleverest nor the most gifted ones, but those who had a goal they were looking forward to during their ordeal. That goal could be anything from being reunited with a loved one to writing a book or getting back to something

---

[21] Ebury Publishing, 2008.

that they had held dear. While they endured the horrors, it gave them the inner strength that kept them alive through the terrible conditions that killed so many.

Such a profound observation is applicable to more common life. People who have a purpose and see meaning in their existence are those who can best withstand the difficulties they face. On the opposite, people who lack vision for their life, such as Lily, are in danger of falling into mental anguish.

Lily heard others in the AA programme who felt as she did. They called it having "a hole in the soul". Like them, she had become used to self-medicating that painful hole by drinking and using drugs. She saw herself as different from addicts who had mostly sought pleasure in substances. Whether she had been drinking or taking drugs, her intention was not to get pleasure.

"It was all about oblivion, wanting to run away, taking an anaesthetic."

She did find sobriety and clarity in AA. She continued her search as finding meaning became her conscious goal. It detached her from her old search for oblivion.

DOUBLE PERSONALITY

Liz, a middle-aged English woman, used to err, trying to make sense of her life. She believed that mental illness was part of the disease of alcoholism and craved "normality".

"I looked in all the wrong places. I felt so empty and lost inside!"

She described the typical double personality that characterises addicts. On one side, she wanted to be normal, and on the other side, she prided herself on being "very cool, very rock'n roll". All the time, beneath her cool façade, she felt painfully lonely, searching and longing to be rescued. She would oscillate between shame when she saw herself as 'lower than' (others) and grandiosity when she saw herself as 'higher than'.

She used to act erratically and was often drunk by breakfast. Most of the time, she felt angry and aggressive.

"People used to call me 'a bumblebee on speed'... My entire twenties were ruled by drink and drugs."

Since being in AA, she has been able to talk honestly about her past abusive behaviours.

"I could be very nasty to people, verbally arrogant, trying to control things. I used vitriolic words... I used to steal money from everybody!"

AA teaches that honesty is a requirement for recovery. AA members have a famous saying about it, "You are as sick as the secrets you keep". They find recovery when they uncover their secrets to others. Liz's very honesty helped her along the recovery road.

ALWAYS RUNNING AWAY

The fears that people endure when they are seriously depressed can lead to procrastination in self-care and basic duties. Addicts commonly see duties such as paying utility bills as big mountains.

Alex, a middle-aged businessman, used to neglect his basic needs of food, sleep, exercise and dentist's appointments. For years, he was also dogged by a fear of lacking financially, compounded by the fact that he never wanted to ask for help.

"I wanted to do everything on my own. It was coupled with a complete inability to take care of myself. I needed to go to the dentist, but I wouldn't. I couldn't handle utilities... I would go to any length to have my own way, like changing jobs or countries... I spent my whole life running away, unable to cope with how I felt."

Running away is a common behavioural pattern for addicts. It is also typical of people who suffer from Borderline Personality Disorder (BPD). BPD, which is part of some addicts'profiles, has even been called "the run-away sickness"[22]. Denial often accompanies it, a refusal to face the fact of being an addict[23].

During his active alcoholism, Alex would not take responsibility for the care of his needs. Then he would get angry because his needs were not met. And he would turn his anger against himself by setting out to drink himself to death.

"I spent fifteen years trying to kill myself."

He was also very impulsive. That affected all his relationships. When he felt resentful, he could get into a rage, suddenly flaring up. In AA, he realised that, in order to manage that problem, he first had to take care of his own needs.

"I think of it as putting on your own oxygen mask before putting one on somebody else. If I do that when I'm with somebody else, my anger isn't going to spill out. For example, right here right now, I've taken care of my stuff this morning, so I'm focused on doing this and not thinking about how you're doing or why you're doing it or 'marking it'...."

---

[22] Reiland R., *Get Me out of Here*, Hazelden, 2004.

[23] 12-Step fellowship members joke about it, saying, "You think denial is a river in Egypt!" ('De Nile' being a colloquial way to say 'the Nile').

By "taking care of his stuff", he meant meditating as well as fulfilling his basic needs. He learned that if he took care of them first, his relationships with others were smoothed like when there is a disturbance on a plane, we are advised to put on our own oxygen mask *before* helping a child or someone else.

"But if I didn't do my stuff, I'd come along and maybe, unbeknown to me, lurking under the surface somewhere, there'd be anger. That's how my life was: lurking under the surface, there was anger. I could ask for something nicely... If I didn't get it, I'd be volcanic!"

As a child, he had been taught religious rules that he understood as demanding perfection. By internalising them, he had become a perfectionist.

When he later fell into alcoholism, his inner critic wondered how he could behave as badly as he did despite his religious faith. He used to be the hardest judge of himself and condemn his actions as well as his lack of action. Identifying as a religious man, he saw himself as fighting a spiritual battle against alcoholism.

He also felt 'emotionally enmeshed' with his work.

"I could not cope with saying no and constantly felt under pressure, stressed and in a hurry."

People who want to please at all costs are unable to say no and that often results in an accumulation of work or 'obligations' with ensuing pressure and stress. For a similar reason, many are always in a rush. They may end up with physical or mental ailments or both.

CARRYING PARENTS' ANGER

Like so many children of alcoholics, Carl was raised in a chaotic home atmosphere where he did not feel loved. Because of it, he thought he was not loveable and even could not love himself.

"I loved my parents, but didn't realise they had the illness of addiction... However much I would ask my dad to stop drinking, he couldn't. He used to drink every night after work. My mum didn't use to drink all the time like my dad. She just had a bad reaction to it. It totally transformed her."

His parents were *functioning alcoholics*. They could put up a good front or hold a job. For a child, having an alcoholic parent who is 'functioning' is extremely confusing.

Carl was puzzled by the constant pretending and lies in which his family lived and the resulting chaos and hypocrisy surrounding him.

"Though I knew they drank too much, at the time I didn't know what it entailed. I had no idea. So, they were 'functioning'... Just about! That's where I would ask God, 'God, why have you given me that? Why have I parents like this? Why? I want normal parents!' On my dad's side, his mother met some Muslim and married again. So, they were Muslim, but my dad didn't participate in that stuff. We would have relatives over, and I remember they would be quite shocked 'cause we had a prayer mat draped on the couch... They weren't too happy! We had to get it off the couch. I remember my mum saying, 'Quick, get it off the couch!' That's how religious we were!"

The children had to participate in the cover-up by quickly helping to hide the prayer mat to conceal the Muslim side from other visiting relatives. In the house, religion was all a show: getting out the prayer mat to please the Muslim relatives when they visited and, when they left, doing what the Muslim religion forbids: eating pork and not only drinking alcohol but abusing it...

The youngest of five children, Carl was given drugs by his siblings from the age of eight. They were all much older than him and thought it was fun. As a typical younger child, he was looking up to the older ones. He missed them when each of his brothers and sisters fled the home atmosphere as soon as they were old enough.

Left alone with his parents, he felt abandoned, lonely and became depressed. To medicate his low feelings, he used the escape route he had learned from his siblings, alcohol and drugs. His acquired habits escalated until he became a heavy user, to the point of inching toward death.

"I was living with an illness that wanted to feed on doom, disaster and negativity."

He could not relate to normal people. He felt like an alien in their presence and used to explode in anger.

"I don't have to scream and shout to show someone I'm angry, but that's how I used to express anger, or just let it build up, build up, build up and then, 'Brrrr! Rrrmm!' like a bomb. And then everyone goes, 'God, what's wrong with you?' Yeah, and I can't turn it off... I can now get angry, tell someone I'm angry, leave the situation, walk away from it and not respond in a bad way. And then I can pray to be relieved from it."

Prayer helped somewhat to relieve him of anger and, to do his part, he learned in AA a strategy which he could use when he still occasionally became angry: he would tell someone about it and avoid trouble by leaving the situation.

WORRY, FEAR AND SHAME

Emma, an Irish woman in her forties, had lived with depression for many years.

"Everything was a big decision, so difficult. I felt overwhelmed with choice. I would worry with a fear of death... obsessed with it."

She attributed her low state to what she called the "dark Catholicism" in which she had been brought up. The rules had made her fearful. The guilt and shame she felt had become triggers for her to drink heavily.

"It was cold and conditional... I was scared!"

Self-loathing usually leads to having the same attitude toward others. Hence, she was judgemental toward people and toward God.

"In my mind, God was a guilt-inducing disciplinarian... I had issues with my father, so I had issues with that 'Father' business."

Many people believe that God is harsh and punitive when they feel guilty because of false teachings or excessive punishment received during childhood. They grow up with a mental representation of God similar to their memory of the person who had punished them harshly. They may cover it up, even from themselves, but be self-critical. Emma was very critical of herself.

"I needed liberation from suffering, that sense of duty and self-deprecation. I would make a prescriptive list of what I wanted to be like and I'd say prayers, not really thinking what they meant."

As long as she held that belief in a condemning God, she had no peace.

FAMILIAR PAIN, FAMILIAR BLAME

Dom still had a childish face in his thirties. He was born to strict, controlling, alcoholic parents and, as a child, experienced that feeling of isolation so frequently found at the root of adult dysfunctions.

"There was not much love. I was hurt. I felt as if I could not talk to anyone. I couldn't trust people. I was very silent, extremely sensitive."

Life outside the home was also difficult. He was bullied at school. School bullies generally target children who are already victims in their homes. They probably sense that victimised children are unlikely to assert and defend themselves.

As a little boy desperately looking for refuge, Dom went to a church. He found comfort in it and decided to take Jesus as his friend. However, as he grew up, he came to the conclusion that his sexuality was incompatible with churchgoing.

"I felt unsafe. The intolerance of established religion drove me away."

Even people with conventional sexuality have been driven away from religion by the narrow-minded attitude of some religious folks about the topic.

After leaving mainstream religion, he continued to consider Jesus as a friend. Later, as a university student, he joined a Christian Union. He initially liked it, but when he became more involved, he found it too strict. He was reminded of his struggles as a young teenager. Again, his sexuality did not fit with religion as he perceived it.

He chose to go out with a different kind of crowd. Then he observed that for that crowd, "...religion was uncool!"

He indulged in various addictive behaviours that soon got out of hand. He drank heavily and his gambling became unmanageable. As a result, he thought he was going insane.

"I thought I was weird. I was addicted to many things: alcohol, cigarettes, overeating, etc..."

He realised that drinking cut him off from his spiritual beliefs.

"I came to a point where drinking was not fun anymore. I did a lot of thinking and would spiral down. I was depressive... Addiction is a serious illness."

Then he took a job. He was very unhappy at work. He was bullied again, this time by his manager. The repetition of what he had endured at school felt painfully familiar.

"I found it extremely stressful."

Paradoxically, it is often easier for those who have had an abusive, traumatic childhood to remain in a familiar situation that reminds them of the past, however hard the situation is, than to attempt to live in a new, better one. They might repeat the difficult patterns they experienced in childhood, unconsciously recreating circumstances similar to those that had hurt them so badly.

"I could put up with years in horrible situations or thoughts. I would anaesthetise myself by drinking. I had a huge tolerance for pain... or so I thought! Now I don't want that kind of pain anymore and I'm glad if I get any kind of pain, I will try to work on it. I know, ultimately, I'm going to have to do something about that anyway, so I might as well do it sooner than later."

When he reflected on it, Dom became aware that there was something wrong with his attitude. It helped him to realise that he had been used to living through very painful situations since childhood. He had tolerated pain until it became extreme.

"All the time, I would blame my family, my manager or anything for what I was going through. I was prickly, angry and opinionated... I would pick up on people looking at me in a funny way. It was awful. I was desperate, thinking about what other people thought of me."

People who are critical of others are usually critical of themselves, sometimes without being aware of it. Dom did not escape this pattern. When he was hurt, he blamed not only others but himself too.

As he followed the guidance of the AA programme, he considered the part he had played in situations in which he found himself. It had a therapeutic effect on him.

It helped him to change, not always the situation, but his depressed feelings about it. He was able to work on his resentments. He learned to stop when he became aware he was blaming others or himself.

He would not stay in a hard place anymore. When he realised he felt resentful, he would do an inventory, examining himself and his motivations and letting go of what he recognised as toxic.

"Sometimes, when I get a big resentment of someone, I write it down and spend an hour with the resentment because it's not always the first answer... That's a very spiritual process. I find inventory[24] almost like a brain-storming process. 'Why is this happening to me?' Then, normally an answer comes. That's quite painful. I usually can't be bothered, but when I feel something is really badly affecting me – it might be something simple like being really jealous of a work colleague 'cause I think they've got an easier life – I just have to go through an inventory. Then the answer comes. First of all, you can't change that. You might want to change it but, generally speaking, you can't change a lot of things you resent...."

---

[24] Doing an inventory of one's life, recent or past, is part of the 12-Step programme.

TO RETAIN

TO DEAL WITH RESENTMENTS, the programme says, "set them on paper".

- Annie accepted being 100% responsible for how she felt. If anything happened that offended her, she kept it in the day.
- John examined his motivations. He realised he was not due happiness.
- Mark sat with his pain. He looked at his part only, not the other person's.

FEELING ALIENATED

- Fred realised he needed others.
- Lily looked for meaning in her life.
- Liz opened up honestly about her secrets.

TO DEAL WITH ANGER

- Alex stopped running away. He also made a point of taking care of his basic needs.
- Carl prayed and told someone about his anger. He avoided trouble by leaving the situation.
- Emma realised God was not critical and judge-mental of her. It helped her to get peace.
- Dom stopped remaining in abusive situations.

Sneak Peek Into Meetings

Richard Farson noted that it was the desperation addicts felt that led them to progress. "Very often, it is the crisis situation that actually improves us as human beings. Paradoxically, while these incidents can sometimes ruin people, they are usually growth experiences."[25]

Indeed, most alcoholics who attend their first AA meeting are motivated by an intense personal crisis.

RELIEF FROM LONELINESS

When Carl's suffering became too hard to bear, he found his way to an AA meeting. He could not endure his pain of loneliness anymore.

"I finally got to my first meeting, overwhelmed by it all, just isolated. I didn't know what to expect, but when I arrived, I felt like, 'Oh, there's hope! These people are like me!'"

When, for the first time in his life, he could identify with other people, he felt a sense of joy. However, he was reluctant to accept the word 'God' when people mentioned it or when he read about it in AA literature.

Children who suffer at the hands of abusive parents often end up copying them and adopting the same

---

[25] Farson Richard, *Calamity Theory of Growth*, quoted in Edith Eger, The Choice, Rider, 2017, p. 229.

attitudes. That was Carl's case. Though he had greatly suffered because of his alcoholic father, he had adopted his views. For years he had taken on the critical attitude about spirituality in which he had been raised. Then in AA, he was pulled between the relief he felt when hearing people share about their lives and his old rejection of any and all references to God.

"When I see, *God, God, God, God*... I think, 'Oh!' Alarm bells start ringing. 'What is going on? What is this place?' But then we'd read some preambles. People say their names and say they're addicts, and then it just hits me. Oh, I've got to cry, trembling, to say my name, and say, 'I'm an addict,' and it just picks the lid off this pressure cooker. It's like, 'I've arrived at last! Can this be? Is there a way out of this?' 'Cause by this time, I'm desperate... So, I felt an overwhelming sense of relief."

Being able to recognise himself in what others said was liberating. Then he would remember his father's old discourse against God and a battle would rage in his mind. That kind of battle is experienced by many adults: they try to remain loyal to their dysfunctional parents despite the abuses they endured at their hands. "People of all ages are... afraid of betraying their parents."[26] They do not realise that it is not really the parents they need to renounce but the disease, the disorder, the dysfunction.

When Carl considered what believing in God would mean for him, he automatically imagined being ridiculed in the same way believers had been ridiculed by his father. It brought back the familiar pervasive feeling of shame, along with the fear of rejection and abandonment that characterises children of alcoholics.

---

[26] *Adult Children of Alcoholics*, World Service Organization, Torrance, California, 2006; p. xxiii.

Despite that, he remained intrigued by the recovery he observed in meetings. He was attracted by the countless stories of people getting better. They kept him coming back.

"So, I came in and I didn't know... 'Higher Power? What is this?' I kept coming in and out because I had a huge resistance to getting well, and the God stuff put me off. I used to keep coming into meetings and back out and do my own research. I would think, 'Look at these steps! What can I take from here? How can I do this stuff?' And I'd see one shaking and then get control and have control back in his life!"

He could not help nor deny noticing how effective AA was for other addicts. He figured it could work for him too. Because of it, he persisted despite his resistance. The events of his life, seen in the light of what he heard in meetings, helped him to face himself more honestly.

What fellows say in meetings can often act as mirrors that might jolt hearers out of their denial.

NO LONGER INSANE

John was intrigued when he saw people's contentment in meetings. It made him question his negative mindset. Though he described himself as a staunch atheist, he observed that the closer people were to their Higher Power, the happier they appeared. The Higher Power seemed to be central not only to sobriety but also to well-being.

"You can almost gauge people's level of contentment from their degree of contact with their Higher Power! Those people who maintain a constant dialogue with their HP – whatever that is – seem to be happier than the people who struggle with it. Intellectually, I struggle with it... I try not to let it worry me too much."

The fact that the AA programme included having a relationship with a Higher Power left him perplexed. He decided to find out how other atheists in recovery managed to stay sober.

"I sought out a well-known atheist and asked him for his point of view. He was a big believer in going to meetings. 'Just do lots of meetings and that will keep you sober!' I pretty much go to a meeting a day anyway, so I have that level of reinforcement on a daily basis."

Attending meetings is indeed an important part of the self-care practices advised in AA. John noticed that no matter what people shared, it could affect him deeply, personally and intimately.

"The Higher Power in the *rooms*[27] cares for me! Actually, you can hear someone who's got a perfectly ordinary story and see how things were hard for them too. So that was opening my eyes about being selfish..."

He was surprised to be deeply touched by some people who he had first judged and classified as ordinary when they described their exceedingly difficult stories. It awoke a feeling of compassion in him. He realised that because of his selfishness, he had closed his heart to others' suffering.

As is commonly suggested to newcomers with no previous spiritual beliefs, he chose to take the AA programme itself as his Higher Power.

"I found it quite easy in my early days to conceive of it as the power of the group or the power of the principles

[27] AA members refer to the places where they meet as 'the rooms'. They rent those rooms often in churches or other public buildings.

behind AA, taking out the personalities. That fulfils a number of criteria. I suppose it fulfils the main HP criteria, which is *a power greater than yourself*."

On top of 'working the programme', observing how satisfied people in AA seemed to be with their lives, spoke to him. He opened his mind to the possibility of changing.

"I am no longer insane. Do I think it's a Higher Power that did that for me? It *wasn't* me! So, it's my starting point. And I toyed with different ideas of what a HP is... I am a work-in-progress."

HOW ABOUT THE FUN IN LIFE?

When Mark first attended AA, he thought he would have to abandon what he considered "the fun" in his life. Then he realised that it was precisely this kind of fun that had led him into trouble. What he heard people share in meetings reminded him that his alcoholism had put him on a path to death.

"They talked about the heart and soul a great deal and they made reference to the inner journey... There is a saying in AA I heard early on, which was 'GOD stands for the Gift Of Desperation'. That put the hook in me. I understood I *had* to have that desperation. I had to have suffered in order to seek."

He used to be torn between fun and spirituality, believing the two were incompatible. Then, he felt a tangible power in meetings that was better than his old idea of fun.

"I tried just to stop drinking and attend meetings and not really explore the spiritual angle because it was going to take me away from having fun in life... but going to meetings was almost like a form of osmosis. And the longer you go, the more you just absorb it...."

People often commented on a certain 'something' or power they felt when listening or speaking during those gatherings. They even remarked that it worked not only during the meeting itself – like a show can bring joy to those who watch or act in it – but also after it. As if it had impregnated the participants, it seemed to follow them in their lives. They described a sort of *anointing of sobriety* they received while together and carried with them when going outside and throughout their everyday life. It would continue to keep them sober through situations that used to trigger their craving for a drink.

THE RIGHT CLUB

In the past, Fred had neglected his need for social contact. His life was transformed when he started attending meetings regularly. For the first time in his adult life, he felt part of a community.

He had never really trusted anybody before. He was surprised when that changed. Like many others, he alluded to the power he felt in meetings.

"It is in the *rooms*. I get help in the rooms, the group of people... To start with, being in a group of complete strangers in a room, there is no trust there. Then, for people who have been isolated for a long time, just being in a group of people could be amazing. You feel you're in the right club... The Higher Power can be in the room. That can be very powerful. I felt it this morning, a feeling that you're in the right place and that you're not alone... Their Higher Power in the room rubs off, or the confidence people have to talk about it. It will be heard by someone on their first day or in their first year. If you repeat the process over and over, it starts to sink in... This is teamwork."

He observed a diversity of backgrounds in the group, and especially those that were very different to his own.

"Some people have had a *good* experience of religion. Their parents are religious. In North London, you get a lot of Irish Catholics... As they say the words 'I'm Catholic', I go 'Pff!' because I know, 'You're going to hell, boy! No two ways about it: you're a *sinner*, so...'"

He laughed at the differences he heard, but he noticed that every newcomer was given a chance and was offered honest social contacts, often for the first time. He found that rewarding.

"Choice isn't so clear in the early days. It's fifty-fifty whether to go to a meeting. Suggestions are key 'cause you can't tell an alcoholic much. He's stubborn, he's arrogant. But given a choice, he'll say, 'Oh yeah, I'd like that one'...."

He knew that the two alcoholics who had started AA had initially become sober with the help of a group of Christians.

"It does have those influences..."

He compared AA to a religion.

"It's like church I guess...."

When tempted to stray and go on a binge, he availed himself of the power of confession in meetings. He learned to deal with situations that might trigger his old compulsion to drink. To avoid yielding to temptation, he talked about it honestly to people whom he knew would not condemn him. He trusted that by telling others about it, he would receive the support he needed.

While Liz opened up about her past shameful attitudes, he opened up about his present triggers. Both heeded the AA warning, *"You are as sick as the secrets you keep"*.

"If you talk about these things, get it in the open, it's not an evil little secret. Otherwise, it would manifest and rot. It'd get worse and worse. But if you're doing the meetings, you're getting support. You're talking about it. There's no build-up of that, 'Oh, I've got to drink!' 'No, you don't!' So, you talk about it and get it out there, bore everyone stupid with the same thing, but if it stops you drinking for that day, it works! And for someone to be brave enough to sit up there and talk about something that's really personal and not feel ashamed – 'We're not judging you at all. It's just good for you to tell us!' – If you start to do that, you feel stronger because... actually, you become powerful. You do become free. Teamwork gives hope and faith. Opening up instead of keeping a plan secret kept me sober. Talking about temptation prevents it from building up. I pick up pointers in meetings. Sharing at meetings makes me feel stronger."

As another way to fight his illness, he practised the part of Step 12 asking to *'carry the message to others'*. To help him do that, he believed he had to be "on top of the meetings", by which he meant going to meetings regularly. There he could meet and help other alcoholics.

BEING A SPECTATOR

In meetings, people describe how they apply different aspects of the programme. It can help others to reflect on their own attitudes. Thus, Lily found help when she heard individuals talk about their prayer life. She wanted to apply what they described, but she felt like a spectator.

"Prayer, what's that? Pray to what? Pray to love? What does that mean? I need to work a bit on my prayers. Why do people pray to something? Is it within or without, or both? A relationship meaning *an exchange*, I need a figure or an object to relate to it."

She still had many questions, but as she did what she could, she progressed in sobriety. It kept her coming back to meetings.

THE POWER THAT KEEPS US SOBER

Attending meetings was not just a necessity for Alex. He enjoyed them. The fellowship he discovered fulfilled his need for social contact, which he had neglected during his years of excessive drinking.

"I need to go, but actually, I like going. I'm glad that motive doesn't matter in AA. The good part of my motive for going to AA meetings is fear: I'm sure I would have a bad end if I didn't go. There are people who don't go and relate more to doing something else. Maybe not for anybody, but for me, there would be difficult times ahead. I am completely convinced that wouldn't work for me. I want a solid foundation on which to go. So, if somebody said to me, 'Oh, you don't need to go anymore!' I would be devastated... I like the people."

Like many before him, he was intrigued by that certain 'something' in meetings. He saw it as a factor in his recovery.

"There's a power in an AA meeting, but I have no idea what it is. I don't even know what created it... Who knows which part of an AA meeting works? We don't know. We don't *need* to know! And it's probably the reason AA is still going because we don't know; because if people knew, they'd want to play around with it. So yes, there is this power that keeps us sober and I couldn't stay sober by myself, so I know it's there."

Like Fred, another reason he attended meetings was that in them, he could find people who needed help.

"The other thing is it's only by going to meetings that you can get the opportunity to help other people."

Helping others is a key part of the AA programme and is often considered as a condition for staying sober.

EVERYBODY AT THE SAME LEVEL

Coming to AA radically improved Emma's mental health. The honesty of the shares [28] lifted her.

"I guess that's an aspect of how the rooms work. Ultimately, we're all in the rooms because we're flawed. We've all done bad things and that does level pride. It makes us all at the same level."

Hearing people talk about their situations in meetings comforted her about her current difficulties. Through that, she also acquired faith in the future, something she had never before experienced.

She found help for her problems when she heard people talking about situations they were going through that were far worse than hers, trusting that things would be all right in the end. It encouraged her to put into perspective whatever circumstances she had to face. If

---

[28] What people say in meetings.

others could be fine while enduring such ordeals, her life did not seem as bad as she had previously thought.

"That is how I got on the right track. It helps when I go to meetings and I hear other people sharing and what they're going through is terrible. It's death! And when I hear them saying they know they're going to be okay – that's how strong their faith is, whatever it's in – that makes me feel better. That makes me feel I can deal with whatever is going on in my life, which is minor in comparison."

Attending meetings resulted in her opening up to a positive belief system. She went from an environment of oppressive religion to one where she felt no discrimination.

"My perception of the Higher Power has changed in the rooms from a God that was kind of *obligatory*. Listening to people has liberated me from dark Catholicism. It's moved me away from that sense of duty, that suffering and guilt. Moving out of the darkness into the light is as different as day and night and a lot better for me... My therapist said that religion needs to be all about love."

Some people find the mixture of rules and tolerance in AA disconcerting. The rules are in place to keep individuals safe and the tolerance shows them they are accepted. Emma particularly appreciated the tolerant aspect of meetings.

Addictions are known to be great levellers, happening to all types and classes. So is the AA programme, even if there are specialised meetings such as for 'Women Only' or other ones where Emma went sometimes.

"There are meetings for agnostics and atheists and I've been to a couple. Because if I'm in an area and there's a meeting on, I'll go to it. It doesn't matter if it is 'Gay-Lesbian' or 'Agnostic-Atheist'. Nobody ever turns around and says, 'But you're not that!' It's just done respectfully. People are respectful of others and no one will ask whether I belong."

PURE PLACES TO PRACTISE

For Dom, attending AA meetings was as important for practicing his faith as prayer or meditation. He observed that meetings worked, even though they could vary greatly. He appreciated their variety and the acceptance of all personal beliefs.

"How come AA meetings work so well? It's because you put your differences aside and just go for the common good. They're very pure places to practise the Higher Power."

He likened AA to a religion with God at the centre.

"For me, AA is like a religion, very much a spiritual path. I'm quite respectful of it... You have to be mindful of what you talk about in meetings, and you don't want to scare off newcomers, but at the end of the day, it's a spiritual, religious program... Sometimes, when you go to a room of AA and you have these people from different backgrounds and different experiences – some of them quite clearly mad, or *were* mad or perhaps people are struggling more – people on different levels, how come they work so well?"

He particularly appreciated the respect people showed for each other during and after meetings.

"The idea is just very nice. You say, 'Thank you'. You say 'Hello' to everybody. Everyone is given a chance to share. The idea is you *do service* together. Even if some patience is needed, even if some go on talking for half an hour, you shouldn't really give any criticism afterwards... There might be a few meetings where it goes a little bit off. You might have heard of meetings where they're very rigid in terms of, 'You have to do this! You have to do that! You have to call two people a day.' I've not found that helpful myself... although it's a broad church. I think it's *like* a church... You get very evangelical churches and very liberal churches, and they probably help people. But for me, it's tolerance that's underpinning it. People don't interrupt. In a word, it's reverence."

Listening to whoever talks without interrupting is one of the rules of 12-Step meetings. It guarantees respect. After meetings, people discuss freely. They have a chance to give and receive more individualised help.

"You listen to somebody and then share back, and you offer to do service. And if someone comes up to say, 'I'm really, really struggling', in a good meeting, people would, as much as possible, try to listen to them, maybe give them phone numbers, maybe say, 'Do you fancy a cup of coffee or something?' and listen to them, and then say, 'But come back!' Initially, I don't believe in smothering them too much, but I believe in saying, 'Come back next week, we'll be there and we'd love to see you next week!' That kind of thing worked for me. And when you know people really want to talk, you might give them your number and they can call and then you feel like you're helping... As an alcoholic, you are supposed to help another one."

One of the AA Traditions[29] is to refrain from mentioning religion or politics. Following it, Dom did not talk about his faith during meetings. Neither did he feel comfortable

---

[29] On top of the 12-Steps, which provide guidance to individuals for personal recovery, the 12 Traditions provide guidance for the conduct of meetings.

talking openly about other parts of his private life in a group.

"In terms of my day-to-day life and relationships, my belief in my HP, I'm not very open about telling people. I don't go around saying, 'Jesus loves you' or anything like that. It's not my style... I'm still very messed up and I still do act out on things that I'm not proud of. I do unhealthy things like swear, things I'm not too happy with..."

Previously, like a lot of people, he had a perfectionist interpretation of religion and it had discouraged him. He was always looking at his faults and thought that he was never good enough. The acceptance he found in AA liberated him from that guilt. The AA programme was simpler and easier to practise than established religion. It had been liberating for him to hear he only had to do it "to the best of his abilities". It gave him permission to be himself at last. It also gave him a chance to have a spiritual relationship with a loving God.

Attending meetings regularly, as helpful as it can be, is not the most important factor in maintaining the 'gift of sobriety'. "With a few exceptions, AA-focused studies show commitment to, and practise of, prescribed AA behaviours is a stronger predictor of later abstinence than sheer frequency of AA meeting attendance."[30]

---

[30] Tonigan J.S., in M. Galanter and L. A. Kaskutas, *Research on Alcoholics Anonymous and spirituality in addiction recovery.*

TO RETAIN

RELIEF FROM LONELINESS

In meetings, Carl found relief from loneliness. Moreover, hearing and seeing AA work for others helped him believe it would work for him too.

POWER TO BE NO LONGER INSANE

John was 'no longer insane'. He attributed this to the power found in AA meetings.
He also observed that people's levels of contentment were related to their relationship with their Higher Power.

MORE THAN FUN

In meetings, Mark discovered something more powerful than what he called "the fun in life" and that he could enjoy more.

TEAMWORK

Fred found himself 'in the right club' where he could open up without fear of being judged.
Teamwork gave him hope in his life and faith to remain sober.

REALISE WHAT NEEDS TO BE WORKED ON

As a spectator, Lily realised she needed to work on her prayer life.

POWER TO KEEP ONE SOBER

Alex felt in meetings a power that kept him sober.
He also found in them people that he could help.

COURAGE TO FACE HARD SITUATIONS

For Emma, seeing everybody at the same level was liberating.
When she heard about some very bad situations experienced by people who had the faith to go through them, it gave her the courage to face her own, which appeared easy by comparison.
Alex also mentioned that it made him see his circumstances as not so hard after all.

CONTACT WITH A HIGHER POWER

For Dom, meetings were "pure places" to practise contact with his Higher Power.
He appreciated the respect and reverence for each other that he found in them.

The Gift of Desperation – how can desperation be a gift?

"**D**esperation can lead to sincere faith that can be of tremendous help in recovery."[31]

Anybody may encounter circumstances that can lead to desperation, whether to do with health, relationships, work, finances, or any area of life. In AA, desperation is seen as a gift because it has led countless members to change their lives. They call it the *Gift Of Desperation*. The use of its initials as an acronym for *GOD* underlines the fact that it can have positive consequences in one's life. It is a gift if it helps one to open up and receive help.

When it brings in an alcoholic the desire to change, he or she might try an AA meeting. Once in an AA fellowship (or in any other 12-Step support group), someone who had previously shut the door to spirituality might accept that programme even though it is a spiritual one.

Like the saying, 'You can take a horse to water, but you cannot make him drink', addicts who don't experience that *Gift Of Desperation* commonly refuse the lifeline AA represents. Such an attitude is also similar to that of the homeless person who refuses the offer of a place to stay, a job or social support. It has to do with sticking to

---

[31] Comment about faith on Matthew 15:22-28, *Life Recovery Bible*, Tyndale House Publishers, Illinois, 2015, p. 1221.

an accepted identity such as a label of "homeless" or "habitually drinking".

Some alcoholics come to AA after being pushed by relatives. Others do so after they have been given the alternative of losing their job. Others still do so after they receive a court order offering attendance to AA meetings as an alternative to a sentence of jail. Whatever motivated them to start, the statistics are the same: one-third of all AA attendees go back to their addictions; one-third keep oscillating between recovery and relapse, and one-third maintain a solid recovery. Interestingly, research shows people who attend AA because of coercion are likely to make as good a recovery as those who freely choose it.

Some people receive the *Gift Of Desperation* when they reach rock bottom – though not everybody gets desperate at that point. Some people stay down. Some even commit suicide rather than looking for help.

Reaching desperation has a positive effect when it pushes the person to seek outside help rather than continue to tread the lonely path. It is truly a gift when it leads someone to look for an outside resource and find AA.

The place of rock bottom is different for each person. One alcoholic reached it simply when his nephew, then just a little boy, told him, "Aren't you ashamed of yourself?" That question, and seeing whom it came from, shamed that man so deeply that he vowed then and there to stop drinking. He joined AA and has been sober since. His motivation might seem weak compared to that of other addicts who hit rock bottom only after having lost everything or being at death's door. Yet, it was strong enough for him to seriously turn his life around

– incidentally it might have had something to do with his Eastern culture: westerners are not generally that sensitive to small children's remarks.

The process of change can be quick or slow, depending on the person and their circumstances.

During the recovery process itself, some AA members get a new occasion to receive the *Gift Of Desperation*.

Annie remained abstinent though she did not seem to have ever been really desperate. In AA, she acquired some contentment, along with sobriety. However, she acknowledged that she still had bouts of depression. She did not allow them to drive her to real desperation though. Her own reasoning kept her in denial of any deeper need. She used AA as a sort of self-service where she chose what suited her beliefs. She had set personal limits on how much she would take from what was on offer and did not attempt to adapt to what appeared too foreign to her.

AA does tell newcomers, "Take what you like and leave the rest", but those who make the most progress avail themselves more and more of the different facets of its programme. Some are content to just remain sober. That already represents a remarkable change. Others want to go further, and that means altering more of their old views.

John kept observing other people's fulfilment and not partaking of it, like the old progressive rock song that said, *'I'm on the outside looking inside'*[32]. Though he wanted the fulfilled life he saw some AA fellows enjoy, his tendency to rationalise, similar to Annie's, kept him

[32] King Crimson, *I talk to the Wind*, from the album, *In the Court of the Crimson King*, https://itunes.apple.com

from getting desperate. He differed from her in the fact that he observed others more closely. Because of it, he noticed that people's level of fulfilment depended on their level of spirituality or openness to it, which he called "their relationship with their HP".

Mark was desperate after the break-up of his relationship with a woman to whom he had grown very attached. When a couple goes through a breakup, one or both might become heartbroken or depressed. Many people try to medicate those low feelings by using antidepressants.

Mark chose to follow the AA programme and his desperation led him to a new level of acceptance. He not only accepted his feelings, but he also accepted other people more. Moreover, he accepted what he saw as his Higher Power's will, even when it was contrary to his. Those were invaluable lessons that changed his attitudes and views about life. With what he called "the help of his Higher Power", he was able to turn his familiar negative mindset into a positive one.

Fred became more flexible, more ready to acknowledge his faults. When he realised his mother was dying, at first he planned to medicate his desperation with "a drink" as soon as she passed away. However, he knew his alcoholism was still extremely dangerous.

Acknowledging his plans in meetings allowed him to get desperate in those moments of temptation. His desperation led him to pray and meditate. Then he found healthy solutions. He adopted the same strategy of sharing what he was going through when he was plagued by nightmares. He, who had been so secretive, found a workable solution in simply telling others about his most intimate trials. He adopted the opposite of his usual reserved ways, and it worked.

Lily was openly searching for the 'right' spirituality while trying to practice both Buddhism and Christianity. Through her practices, she found a degree of satisfaction, but that mixing of the two kinds might have been what kept her from experiencing the depth of spirituality she desired. She probably would have been more likely to find it if she were desperate.

Alex regularly went through five-year stages, at the end of which he hit bottom. Every time, desperation brought him back up, and he could apply more AA principles to his life. Those periods helped him to keep learning and growing.

Liz acquired the type of trust that comes after desperation. She recounted an unfair situation she and her family had endured. It had brought her to the end of her rope. As she applied the programme, she became able to accept that situation as part of a bigger plan. Later, that plan unfolded for her good and the good of her whole family.

"Just stand back and see the bigger picture! It's difficult when you're in the middle of something. A year and a half ago, we had a big problem with our neighbours. We have sons of the same age, six years old. They were in a playgroup together, and very quickly they were looking at each other's willies – an apparently perfectly normal behaviour for small children. But the father of that family called Social Services and said our son had sexually abused their son. It was very big, huge! Police intervention! It was frightening and it made me very angry as well… And a year on, we found out they'd invented the whole thing to try to get moved to a bigger flat! It was incredibly painful, but there were moments in that when I was able to go, 'Do you know what? It hasn't finished yet: stand back and wait for the bigger picture, just wait for the bigger picture….' Not always… most of the time, I had images of stabbing them in the eyes and doing… really unspeakable things because I was so angry; but as a direct result of that, we decided our son needed therapy. I found a child psychologist in the rooms in AA. We went to see him at the Addiction Centre, where he worked part-time. My husband came too. He talked to my husband, asking if he had issues with alcohol… Anyway, my husband's now in recovery. That maybe would have happened, but it would have taken longer, and we might not have the family we have today… We might have even split up before it got there. So, as a result, it was all right in the end. It was horrible at the time, but something very good and positive came out of it."

When the truth came out, the affair was closed. Meanwhile, she had learned about trust. She believed if she trusted her Higher Power, whatever difficulties she might go through, things would always work out for good in the end.

Carl had the *Gift Of Desperation* when he had to deal with his pain over the imminent death of his beloved mother. Very upset, he felt he could not handle it without constantly praying and meditating. Then, he received a new perspective on life. It became more enjoyable than just the sobriety with which he had been content for a while. It had taken time and grief, but he finally adopted some of the deeper AA principles he had initially rejected. When he accepted them wholeheartedly, his life blossomed.

Of all the AA members interviewed here, Emma was probably the one who held the simplest beliefs. Having lived a life of depression, a *Gift Of Desperation* led her to keep things simple. She had a strong faith, wholly trusting in a Higher Power that she described as "in the sky", always looking out for her, "even on bad days".

As a child, Dom had sought refuge in a church from his sad life, feeling trapped between a cold, alcoholic family and a school where he was bullied. In the church, he did find faith, but as a teenager, was driven away from organised religion when he felt judged by it. As an adult, after he had acquired several addictions, desperation drove him to AA. There he found acceptance and was able to grow spiritually.

TO RETAIN

WITHOUT DESPERATION, PROGRESS CAN BE LIMITED

Rationalising can keep one from getting desperate. The absence of desperation might limit progress, as seen in Annie's current state of mind.

Being open about what causes others' contentment, as was John, can lead to growth.

Though Lily was somewhat content with doing diverse religious practices, that seemed to keep her from getting desperate. Sober now, she was still searching, desiring greater fulfilment.

DESPERATION CAN TURN A NEGATIVE MINDSET INTO A POSITIVE ONE

Desperation over the breakup of an intimate relationship led Mark to acceptance. His old negative mindset was then turned into a positive one.

DESPERATION CAN LEAD TO SOLUTIONS

Fred's desperation over a difficult situation led him to pray and meditate. He found a healthy solution to his dilemma: sharing it with others in meetings. He then found he could apply that to other difficulties he encountered.

DESPERATION CAN LEAD TO GROWTH

Alex went through seasonal periods of desperation that led him to learn and progress.

Desperation brought Dom to find acceptance and growth in AA.

DESPERATION CAN LEAD TO FAITH AND TRUST

After getting desperate, Liz acquired faith and trust that even very tough situations would work out for good in the end. Subsequently, she observed that they did.

Emma's desperation led her to have a strong, simple faith and trust in her Higher Power.

Carl became desperate over the imminent death of a loved one. As a result, he received a faith he never had before and a more joyful perspective on life.

Applications of the 12-Steps

This chapter provides examples of how the AA interviewees applied the 12-Step programme to their lives.

Note: 12-Step Fellowships such as Narcotics Anonymous (NA), Overeaters Anonymous (OA), Co-Dependents Anonymous (CoDA) and others replace the word 'alcohol' with the name of their substance or behavioural addiction. Alternatively, it may simply be replaced by 'our problems'.

STEPS 1 TO 3: SURRENDERING

Step 1:   We admitted that we were powerless over alcohol – that our lives had become unmanageable.
Step 2:   We came to believe that a power greater than ourselves could restore us to sanity.
Step 3:   We made a decision to turn our will and our lives over to the care of God as we understood Him.

STEPS 4 TO 9: FACING ONESELF AND TAKING RESPONSIBILITY

Step 4:   We made a searching and fearless inventory of ourselves.

Step 5:   We admitted to God, to ourselves and to another human being the exact nature of our wrongs.

Step 6:   We were entirely ready to have God remove all these defects of character.

Step 7:   We humbly asked God to remove our shortcomings.

Step 8:   We made a list of all persons we had harmed and became willing to make amends to them all.

Step 9:   We made amends to such people wherever possible, except when to do so would injure them or others.

STEPS 10 TO 12: A PROGRAMME FOR LIFE

Step 10:   We continued to take personal inventory, and when we were wrong, promptly admitted it.

Step 11:   We sought, through prayer and meditation, to improve our conscious contact with God, praying only for knowledge of His will for us, and the power to carry that out.

Step 12:   Having had a spiritual awakening as the result of these steps, we tried to carry this message to others and to practise these principles in all our affairs.

People who are anxious or depressed, like substance addicts, may or may not be ready to admit they need help to cope with their daily life. However, anyone can find help by practising the methods that 12-Step Fellowship members apply with success.

Step 1 demands acknowledgement of powerlessness. Powerlessness shows in the failure of attempts addicts made to stop their destructive habit(s). AA members start by admitting they cannot control their lives.

Next, for Step 2, they need to recognise that outside help is available.

Step 3 challenges them to accept that help.

A known summary of those three steps is, "I can't. God can. Let Him".

Steps 4 to 7 can be pictured as ploughing the field of a person's heart. By examining what has really been going on, rocks of hardness can be recognised and discarded.

The 4th Step starts the deep work of making an inventory of one's life. That inventory might include not only the faults but also the qualities of the person.

For Step 5, this inventory is shared with a trusted person.

Steps 6 and 7 ask people to become willing to let go of their character defects 'to the best of their ability'. The programme does not demand perfection but only to act the best way one can. That makes it possible for anyone willing to try it.

As the ground of the heart becomes more malleable, deeper soil can be accessed for Steps 8 and 9. The time comes for addicts to recognise that they have hurt not only themselves but also others, particularly those closest to them – parents, spouses, children, or friends. At that stage, the programme includes acknowledging wrong-doings and toxic behaviours.

At Step 8, individuals search their memory for situations and names of people they have harmed.

For Step 9, they seek out those people and make amends to them as long as it is safe to do so for all involved.

Step 10 reminds people, as a way of life, to keep observing and making an inventory of their life daily, again *to the best of their ability*. Its second part shows a way to get regular spiritual cleansing with the application of making amends whenever they are relevant.

To practise prayer and meditation as demanded in Step 11, some people use a specific kind of spirituality or religion. That was Dom's case with Christian spirituality. Lily tried to apply both Christianity and Buddhism. Some do not think they need to go through any religion. Annie and Fred are among those.

The first part of Step 12 requires carrying the AA message of recovery to other alcoholics. The second part asks people to make a daily practice of the Steps. Concert pianists have to faithfully practise their art daily to keep mastering it. It is even more important for those in recovery to practise their programme regularly since it affects their whole life. This is more than an art, as beautiful as that art might be. It can be seen as their ultimate work of art.

APPLYING THE STEPS

At the start of her recovery process, Step 2 was a great hurdle for Annie to pass because the phrase "restore to sanity" implied that she was insane. Even though she had been sectioned in a psychiatric ward as a suicidal alcoholic, she could not face her 'insanity'. Because she was in denial about her mental state, she did not really accept that she needed to be restored to sanity.

This had repercussions on the rest of her interpretations and applications of the Steps. For example, when asked to choose a Higher Power for Step 3, she did not take it seriously.

"A 'power greater than ourselves' didn't mean anything to me! What could be greater than me?"

She did not realise the grandiosity behind her question, nor the fact that grandiosity was also behind her mindset.

Although John had also been mentally ill, he was ready to admit it. He knew that having been dual diagnosed translated into AA language as insanity. As a result, he was open-minded about the meaning of the Steps and ready to recognise he needed a power greater than himself. He first simply accepted his AA meeting as representing that power.

"I can use an AA group as a Higher Power sometimes."

However, when he thought about it more, that did not completely satisfy him.

"To call an AA group 'God' is slightly weird, and obviously not particularly consistent with the idea of a Creative Spirit, or Spirit of the Universe, or other phrases they use in the Book[33]."

He regularly recited the prayer suggested in the AA book that went with Step 3, believing it reinforced his sobriety. At the same time, puzzled by it, he wondered how it could work.

"I'd say the Step 3 prayer, 'God, I offer myself to Thee. Take away my difficulties, that victory over them may bear witness to those I would help of Thy Love, and Thy Way of life.' That makes it quite difficult: you then have to start thinking, 'But what is Thy Way of life?' What does that mean?"

---

[33] Alcoholics Anonymous aka Big Book.

He heard the interpretation of a prayer that provided a satisfying answer. That prayer went with Step 11.

"Someone shared at the meeting that the Step 11 Prayer [*asking each morning in meditation that our Creator shows us the way of patience, tolerance, kindliness and love*] was God's way of life and also the Francis of Assisi's Prayer[34]. Actually, as a set of goals, that's pretty good!"

Francis of Assisi's prayer is quoted in the book *AA 12 Steps and 12 Traditions* [35]. Adapting it as a set of goals helped him to see it as fitting with his beliefs.

Applying the universal laws behind the 12-Step programme worked well in Mark's life. He could increasingly follow his intuition. Intuition, or *in-tuition*, literally means learning from within and that is what he did.

"It was studying and doing the 12 Steps that gave me the insight to feel my instinct, the inner thing when it comes to making a decision."

UK drug rehabilitation centres routinely take their clients to 12-Step meetings as part of their treatment. After his time in one of those centres, Fred went on a six-week alcohol binge. When he emerged, he remembered what he had learned in meetings.

"Right: Step 1. And that's when I got it. It's made me realise I can't do it. It took that relapse for me to realise that I can't do it. It did me a favour; a very easy decision: I just can't do it alone."

---

[34] *Saint Francis' Prayer is:* 'Lord, make me an instrument of your peace; where there is hatred, let me sow love; where there is injury, pardon; where there is discord, union; where there is doubt, faith; where there is despair, hope; where there is darkness, light; and where there is sadness, joy.' It is known as the 11th Step prayer.

[35] *AA 12 Steps and 12 Traditions*, General Service Office, 1953.

Amy Carmichael wrote a poem entitled *In acceptance lieth peace* [36]. Acceptance is an important part of AA practices. Though Fred's set of beliefs differed from those suggested by the AA programme, he found peace in accepting what he could. In his words, he went "from insanity to serenity".

His desire for alcohol was lifted. Later, despite his atheistic views, he reacted positively to Step 2.

"Well, you do *'come to believe'*."

He had been working in a natural environment for a long time and was in awe of it. Nature was the closest representation he had of a Higher Power. In that, he was, unknowingly, a living sample of the Scripture that says, "For ever since the world was created, people have seen the earth and sky. Through everything God made, they can clearly see His invisible qualities – His eternal power and divine nature. So, they have no excuse for not knowing God." [37]

Step 3 presented Fred with an important choice. He could decide to carry on believing in nature as a Higher Power or to believe in something higher. He chose to go along with the programme while retaining his personal interpretation of it.

"Taking the suggestions and using them makes it easier... But it's a God of *my* understanding."

He used some of the initialled acronyms of God regularly cited in AA as reminders.

"It's a good influence, all these analogies: *'Good Orderly Direction'*, *'Group Of Drunks'* [38]... We use 'God' in

---

[36] Amy Carmichael, *In Acceptance Lies Peace*, Key-4-Quoting & People, wordpress.com, 2013 (however, the site is no longer up).

[37] *Life Recovery Bible*, Romans 1:20.

[38] *'Good Orderly Direction'* or *'Group Of Drunks'* are used in AA as acronyms for GOD. They are often appropriated by those who, at their start in the programme, choose AA as their Higher Power.

the *Serenity Prayer*. It doesn't hurt anyone, really... There *is* a Higher Power bigger than me, so I can cope."

He also used meditation, as recommended in Step 11, to face his problems.

"If anything's worrying me, the problem can be alleviated almost immediately with a bit of meditation. It's a routine, very quick but sincere. So, it's helping me along, giving me a push here and there, telling me almost directly that 'No, that was not a wise decision.' I must apologise immediately. It keeps you in check... If you're mean to animals, for example, you don't do that any longer! Your attitude changes. It's right."

This practice helped him remain calm even when he found himself in chaotic or risky situations that previously would have triggered his drinking.

He believed, as stated in the 12th Step, that he had to help other alcoholics in order to fight his own illness. He saw it as a way to turn his addiction into an asset. It gave him a reason to live a more meaningful life than he had ever experienced.

"I did teleservice last night, and I helped a few people. I'll never see them again, but that's part of it. I feel better this morning for no particular reason. You just feel right. This is the plan. And it encourages you to do more. You feel of use. *I* may choose who I want to help or not, but in teleservice, you pick up the phone and you don't know who you're gonna get. So, it deflects the ego."

Like many others, he saw the principles behind the AA programme as universal laws from which anyone could benefit.

"If you apply AA procedures to most things, you can deal with absolutely anything! It's universal. It's been proved time and time again. That's why there are so many Anonymous groups... There're some for everyone."

Alex's religious fervour had not helped him to recover from his alcoholic habit. For years he had wondered why and been confused. In AA, he was liberated from those feelings when he learned he did not have to have strict religious beliefs.

"I think the gentleness of AA's approach is in just 'came to believe'. You don't have to believe now. Just accept that it's a process. 'Came to believe that a power greater than us could restore us to sanity.' It's really gentle. It's not intrusive, it's not evangelical, it's not oppressive. It doesn't have any of the stigmas that lots of religious organisations have. It's God with all the stigmas taken out, so it's palatable even to atheists and agnostics."

Giving people time to 'come to believe' is a gentle way to guide them to spirituality. It may help not only those who had no faith in God but also those with a religious background who had a goal of perfectionism, which is often accompanied by a feeling of shame.

Like Fred, Alex reflected on the universal laws that linked 'working the Steps'[39] with the *AA Book*'s promises of recovery. Among those, he thought particularly about the one that supported Step 12.

"What Lois[40] observed seems to me to be some kind of universal law: *You've got to give it away to keep it.* It's a wonderful way of putting it; working with other people is the way that you stay sober! And it's not just the way you

---

[39] Expression commonly used to mean following the 12 Steps in life.
[40] Wife of Bill Wilson (aka Bill W.), one of the two AA founders. Lois founded AlAnon, a 12-Step fellowship group for family members and friends of alcoholics.

stay sober... Well, I speak for myself: the best way for me to accept my lot is to think about the lot of other people that I know well in the fellowship... Just even being a friend!"

He observed that, though the principles behind AA had been known for a long time, the way they were presented and used was new.

"A lot of these things that Bill Wilson came up with, of course, they existed! He didn't really invent anything, a bit like Steve Jobs didn't invent anything, but he packaged them up, and cleverly. So obviously, the idea of prayer and meditation wasn't new. Working with other people, that's not new. Lois observed the law that you have to give in order to keep. And you could make an argument and say that the 12 Steps are based on Christian principles, but the brilliant bit of packaging is that you don't have to believe in Christianity to accept it! And I don't think AA would have worked if it weren't for these brilliant words, 'God as we understood Him'. If it were God it was selling, huge numbers of people wouldn't go."

On the topic of finances, Alex, remembering he always had problems, took AA's financial organisation as a model to plan his own. AA does not demand its members to pay for the upkeep, but there are bills, such as for the rental of rooms and publications. People contribute as they can and AA is fully self-supported. Financially well-organised, it does not incur debts. An AA tradition demands each group has a prudent reserve for needy days.

"Once upon a time, my way of managing my work was not through an HP but through asking, 'Have I enough money in the bank to pay the bills?' If I have, then I'm fine. Now, I try to have a balance, so I borrowed an idea from AA: I have a *prudent reserve* because I'm self-employed, designed to cover my expenditure. If there's no work for a while, then I trust that if I do the right things, it'll be okay. I don't have to figure it all out, work, work... Before I came to AA, I thought, 'What I need is enough money to last me the rest of my life', and very few people manage that. The reality is you don't need to do that. You just need to let go and say, 'Well, I can pay the bills today. We've got enough to eat, there's nobody chasing me looking for money. I don't owe anybody any money.' I owed money every day for 35 years and now I don't. With my work life, I try to trust more... So, it's in my work life, I would say, there has been the most dramatic change. This was something I just struggled with so much! Today, I can do it."

Liz decided to keep trusting through whatever may be her life difficulties. On the other hand, she believed she needed to do her part.

"When you do Step 3 and hand your life, will and all to the care of God as you understand Him, that should be everything. The Steps are a *design for living*. They should work for everything."

The AA programme is a combination of reliance on a Higher Power and proactive work.

"There is a bigger plan... But it doesn't always work out that way. I have built up my character over 40 years and so it's difficult to then go, 'Oh, it's going to be fine, this is HP stuff.' I worry. I do try to make things work out a certain way at times. I also realise it's all very well trusting and having faith in an HP, but if I don't put in the work, it doesn't mean anything."

For Carl, Step 1 was the easiest and he accepted responsibility for his recovery.

"This was 10 years ago and I got my Step 1. It's easy, 'I'm an addict. I accept that. I surrender. I'm going to do whatever this programme tells me to do 'cause I don't want to use drugs anymore. I'm cleaning myself.' And then my thinking shifted, and I was grateful that my mind had shifted. Step 1 was amazing."

However, after Step 1, it took him a long time to fully accept Step 2. *Coming to believe* happened slowly and progressively. Suffering and desperation played important parts in it.

Many people who are not alcohol or drug-dependent have a similar blockage to Carl's against recognising a Higher Power.

"I baulked at Step 2 because it was about God and it was a struggle! Step 2 was difficult. 'I know that I'm going to have to tell people that I did this stuff thoroughly... I'm never going to have to use again. That's guaranteed. That's what I want!' But because I was thinking of God, I didn't get the stuff thoroughly... I just struggled with that step."

When he was a child, his father, who saw himself as a good socialist, was angry at religion. His interpretation of what Jesus said had profoundly affected Carl.

"He spoke about Jesus being the first socialist. Everyone thought he was the Son of God because when He spoke the Sermon on the Mount with the 5,000, what He said was so beautiful... Not everybody could hear, so they had to whisper and tell everybody what He was saying. And everyone said, 'Who is this guy?' Then they said, 'He must be the Son of God!'"

As his father had told him, Carl thought that the Son of God 'idea' had been made up by the crowd who was listening to him at the time.

"My dad said, 'He was the first socialist 'cause he wanted to share stuff out, so we're all gonna eat, we're all gonna drink!' I liked that. Maybe we'd say, 'He's a good man'. So, I grew up a bit agnostic. I wouldn't want to totally shut the door and say I was an atheist because I sat on the fence."

The reason for that was that he had attended a Church of England school. There, as he became aware of Christianity for the first time, he contemplated the possibility of the existence of God. He thought, "There must be something, a sort of God."

As he grew up, the unhappy home atmosphere took its toll on him, and he questioned it.

"I would say, 'Maybe there is no God! If there were a God, why am I in this situation?' And I would look at war and think of starving children and I'd say, 'Why would God let people suffer?' I'd find that quite hard. And I grew up in a time where a lot of people would stop going to church. Churches were shutting and being converted into flats. Things were changing. Then there was school and hearing about Darwin and evolution, people saying, 'The Bible is just a story'. When I was a kid, it was like, 'What is this? Is it this or is it that?' That caused a lot of doubt!"

Though he wanted to accept how he saw AA helping others, he had a hard time making it fit with his mindset. Then the unpredictable happened, which drove him to take the plunge.

"I had a dream halfway between my Step 2 and my Step 3. Something happened in my dream. And I woke up and I thought, 'Do you know what? That's okay, it doesn't matter. I just want to get well. It doesn't matter about God. I can... It doesn't matter!' Then it shifted, it didn't matter I didn't believe in God. I just had to keep doing this stuff. And I was thinking, 'I came to believe, *came to believe*!' It didn't say I believe or will do automatically!"

He took on what AA had to say, no matter what he felt about it. Then his choice to believe overrode his reasoning.

"From that time, I do believe in the programme. Nothing's going to happen till that happens. Individuals can go to meeting after meeting... Have I still got a reservation in my head? It doesn't matter! I've been restored to a certain amount of sanity."

Later, the practice of Step 11 worked in a situation where he was desperate. He had learned to use his will in AA, but it took a deep crisis for him to have his greatest learning experience. He first had to receive the *Gift Of Desperation*. That happened when he realised that his mother, to whom he was extremely attached, was about to die.

"My mum got ill, and I had to look at my programme. 'What can I do to help myself? I need some help! Where am I not applying the foot to the pedal? Where am I not working my programme best?' It's Step 11! I need to improve my *conscious contact*!"

The support he had found from others in AA was not sufficient to alleviate his pain anymore. He needed support from a higher source. Prayer and meditation were the remedies he took against despair.

"I was distraught. I had to pray and meditate, pray and meditate...."

He understood that, in order to be congruent, he needed to have the will to apply the principles of the programme.

"And so, I did. I prayed for my mum, praying, praying, meditating and praying. I had to because I was falling apart...."

Even in that desperate state, he experienced other positive effects of applying the 12-Step principles.

"And not at one stage did I ever think a drink or a drug would help! The programme doesn't shield me from life unfolding. It doesn't shield me or give me superpowers to make well the people I love. And, being sensitive, I feel stuff more. I needed to tap into this HP. I needed to think, 'I'm not alone. It's going to be all right!' and that my mum would be looked after. So, I prayed and prayed and prayed for that, and I meditated."

When he was most distraught, he suddenly felt a reassuring presence, the source he had been seeking.

"And then I knew I would get through whatever happened. So, it clearly made this connection with my HP bigger... That's the way things happened."

For the first time in his life, he truly accepted God as *the* Higher Power. He had found profound healing in applying Step 11.

"I felt a deep connection where I'd never felt connected... When I took some drugs, it made me feel connected with some human beings, but without it, I didn't. I had never made that connection before. It's only in recovery, after a while, that slowly, slowly, this is being revealed to me through working the Steps."

It had taken an extreme crisis for that staunch agnostic to go to Step 11 as to a lifesaver. At that point, he prayed with all that was in him. It resulted in a spiritual connection, which brought him the peace he needed.

Dom showed through concrete examples how applying the Steps in his daily life had helped him go through everyday difficulties, bringing him balance and satisfaction.

He reached a point in his life where he was ready to take the first Step.

"My understanding is that Step 1 is 'admission of powerlessness, our life has become unmanageable'. For me, it's to say I just cannot do this on my own. I've really tried. It might be stopping drinking, but it might be other things as well... There are probably little steps more, little journeys in the way, but once you admit your powerlessness, if you have any understanding of faith, it becomes clear that you must do certain things. And they might be very foreign, alien or difficult, like praying or meditating."

He understood Step 2 as an exchange in which he would acquire trust.

"Step 2, for me, is really about having faith that, if I do some spiritual things, I will get results, even though I might not be there right now and I might be in a lot of pain."

With the decision to take Step 3, he committed himself to do his part, which was to turn his will and his life over to the care of God.

"Step 3 is *making a decision*, basically saying, 'I'm going to do something different'."

Those first three Steps were his wake-up call.

"It's like coming to the realisation that on my own, I can't do anything because experience has shown that I failed utterly."

Working Step 4 helped him to take responsibility for his problems.

"Step 4 is an important one. It's an inventory of oneself, a big step. It's looking at all the problems I have in my life, putting aside what other people do, saying, 'Where have I been responsible for them?' And that's difficult at first, very difficult!"

He compared Step 5 to the Catholic sacrament of confession.

"The sharing is a very common spiritual thing as well – the confession they have in Catholic places – the idea being that your thinking might not be the best. It's to tell another person about it, to share all of that with someone else."

He described a fundamental key to progress: to stop blaming others and take responsibility for one's own life. In the 12-Step programme, people talk about 'the blame game'.

"It's important you don't blame the other. I can blame my manager, my family; I can blame anything for what I am going through, but that's not helpful because, presumably, I've done it all the time. And this inventory Step is all about saying, 'How have I let these things happen to me?'"

For Steps 6 and 7, he applied the work he had done in the preceding two steps.

"Steps 6 and 7, in the sense of 'Being entirely ready' and then 'Asking God to remove character defects', are very similar in a way. But I normally find them after doing a lot of inventory. I might say, 'I'm sensitive, jealous, insecure, fearful'. Those keep coming up through the inventory process… Saying prayers to the HP helps."

For him, Steps 8 and 9 were about doing things in new ways, as opposed to his past impulsive ways. When he acknowledged toxic patterns of thinking and behaving and made his amends to those he had offended, he was rewarded with peace of mind.

Taking an inventory of his daily life, as Step 10 asks, helped him continue to deal with habitual unhealthy attitudes, such as resentment or jealousy.

"This is saying, after some consultation with a Higher Power, or God, 'How can I do differently?' The Steps are very much spiritual and heart knowledge. The head knowledge is what you've done before. It doesn't work. The good thing about making amends is that it's a miraculous way of getting happiness, joy and closeness to the HP because, like it says in the Big Book, once you're halfway through making those amends, you become close to the HP and handle things differently. The whole flavour of life changes, the whole experience of life. Step 10 is continuing to do it on a daily basis, which I do as much as possible... Sometimes I don't, sometimes I do. One thing very important is to share when something happens and not keep it in. Step 11 is: 'increase your knowledge of the HP'. The 12 Steps are really a way to get close... I do that regularly. I use two religions at the moment, Christianity and Buddhism."

The 12-Step programme is not only about repairing what is or was wrong with one's attitudes but also about applying its different facets wherever needed and helping others to benefit from it.

"Step 12 is about *carrying the message to people who still suffer* and *practising it in daily life*. I tend to do that, practise in my daily life as much as possible."

TO RETAIN

Step 1 was the easiest for Carl. Recognising that he was powerless, he surrendered. Step 2 happened slowly for him, but when it did, it overrode his doubts.

For Dom, Step 1 meant that he could not make it on his own. He saw Step 2 – coming to believe – as an exchange in which he acquired trust. For him, the first three Steps meant doing things differently.

For Alex, Step 2 was a gentle process. He found the programme's absence of strictness liberating, particularly from a feeling of shame that had derived from his religious perfectionist goal.

Step 1 was difficult for Annie because she did not see anything abnormal in her past behaviours. When she reached Step 3, her grandiosity blocked her from acknowledging any power higher than herself.

John also identified as an atheist. When he came to Step 3, he used recommended prayers to "offer [himself] to God", even though he did not quite relate to them.

Fred saw Step 3 as a choice he had to make between nature and something higher. He chose something higher, but it had to be "a God of [his] understanding".

Liz, after handing over her life "to the care of God" in Step 3, felt she also needed to do her part and "put in the work".

When Dom took an inventory of his life for Step 4 and what he compared to the Catholic sacrament of confession for Step 5, he stopped blaming and took responsibility for his problems. After praying, he felt ready for Step 6 and Step 7. Doing a daily inventory, as is asked in Step 10, helped him to continue dealing with unhealthy attitudes. For his daily life practice, he found balance and satisfaction in using both Christianity and Buddhism. It is interesting to note that for him, who acknowledged having a relationship with God, this seemed to work well, whereas for Lily it was not satisfying.

To practise Step 11, John usually prayed the Prayer of Saint Francis of Assisi, interpreting it as a set of goals.

When Carl went through a deep crisis, he remembered Step 11 and used both intense prayer and meditation. As a result, he made a spiritual connection and received a new peace.

Fred particularly liked the meditation part of that step. It allowed him to find calm in chaotic situations that previously would have triggered him. He seriously took in the part of Step 12 that asks one to help others. That gave him a meaningful life and he felt it kept him sober.

Overall, Mark felt 'working the 12 Steps' helped him be more intuitive in his life choices.

Interviewees as different as Mark, Alex or Fred perceived the 12 Steps to be the expression of universal laws that could be applicable to anyone.

Recovery Practices: Sponsors and Sponsoring, Gratitude, Prayer and Meditation

SPONSORS AND SPONSORING

One of the ways to carry the message, as required in Step 12, is to *sponsor* someone.

An AA sponsor is someone who helps another or others to apply the programme in their life. It is an essential part of working the Steps. Everyone who comes to AA is encouraged to find a sponsor, someone to be guided by within the recovery work, and with whom to communicate regularly. People usually choose someone with whom they have an affinity. One is always free to change sponsors if needed.

From his first days in AA, Carl was intrigued when he heard other people talk about their recovery. He wanted the same but was not ready to let go of his independence. For a long time, he resisted anybody who tried telling him what to do. That resistance included looking for a sponsor.

In AA, no one is coerced. Each person learns at his or her own pace. People come to realise what is best for them and to progress as they discern lessons shared in meetings and apply them to their lives.

To become teachable, they might have to overcome their grandiosity. When Carl relates his beginning in AA, he describes that typical attitude.

"I didn't want a sponsor. I didn't want to call anybody. But people were saying, 'It's God's will.' God? What I'd feel like saying is, 'Get lost, man. I don't want God's will. I want my will. I run this show here!' But then, so and so is saying, 'Look at where they ended up'... 'Look at where *I* ended up! What show are you running? It's a comedy show or it's a disaster! It's a black comedy!' By the time I wanted recovery, I'd had numerous relapses. And when I got desperate enough to ask for someone to help me, they told me what I should do. Then I was ready. I could listen; I could hear them. I was teachable."

Emma's sponsor taught her how to handle her problems. It helped her adopt a new attitude of acceptance.

"My sponsor will always tell me to read 'Acceptance was the answer'. It's page 417, just a paragraph or two.[41] That's basically saying, 'Everything is the way it's supposed to be.' And if there's something wrong, you have to look at yourself. That helps me. God has arranged everything to be this way. This is the way it's supposed to be... You have a problem with that? You are the problem! It simplifies things, rather than being like, 'Oh no! If this person did this and this person did

---

[41] From the *AA Book*.

that....' No! You just know something's wrong and that's when you look inside. It's more systematic. You're feeling upset or angry, and you think everything is the way it's supposed to be, so it's with yourself. At that point, if you want to feel better, you can sit down, write something, think about that, and just work it out. It's also restored my faith in my connection with my HP and other people as well, that other people will listen and help, whereas it was not really what I had experienced before."

Being helped by a sponsor was key to Dom's recovery. He knew he could only work well with a tolerant sponsor by whom he could feel accepted.

"I had to have a lot of help to get to this level. I found someone who's sponsoring me... He's extremely messed up in his own way, but he understands me completely. We're both messed up and we're going forward in our own ways. He never judges, which is important... I will say, 'Well, I've done it!' and he'd say, 'Okay, I understand. I'm also an addict. I understand, but let's pray about it, pray and try again next time'. And that's what I need...."

That attitude was very different from the critical one he had endured in the past. Because of how he had been treated, he had not been able to accept himself as he was. In AA, he found a sponsor who was on a similar path to his. The fact that they had the same issues helped Dom accept himself.

The 12-Step programme does not exclude professional help. Dom also regularly saw a therapist. When it came to spirituality, though, he preferred talking to his sponsor.

"I find therapy very useful and that's not very religious, but then my sponsor is quite a religious person. I have a good, helpful therapist, but my sponsor can suggest spiritual stuff that speaks my language. So, it's a bit of both and I feel nowadays that I'm more mature and I can handle life."

WHAT THEIR SPONSORS BROUGHT THEM

Carl, being very independent, did not initially want a sponsor. He had to go through many relapses before he was desperate enough to ask for someone's help. It showed he had become teachable.

Emma's sponsor helped her to adopt an attitude of acceptance of her problems and to look at her part in them.

Dom, having felt significant condemnation in his past, believed he needed a sponsor who would be particularly tolerant. Knowing his sponsor had similar issues helped him to accept himself. He also appreciated being able to talk to him about spirituality, which he did not feel he could with his therapist.

ABOUT GRATITUDE

It has been said every problem starts as a solution to another problem. The problem with resentment starts as a tentative solution to pain. However, not only does it fail to truly heal the hurt, but it makes it worse.

Research has shown that the practice of gratitude had a pacifying effect on the brain. It makes people feel more in control, happier, and more resilient. It improves relationships.

Richard Rohr practises gratitude as a remedy, a counter-poison to use against resentment. "In my experience, if you are not radically grateful every day, resentment almost always takes over."[42]

---

[42] Rohr R., *Breathing Under Water*, SPCK Publishing, 2006, p. 65.

Resentment is a recurrent problem for those striving with addiction. Gratitude, as an antidote to it, has become an integral part of the AA programme. Like Richard Rohr, those in recovery from alcoholism, who were subject to negative thinking, anger, etc., testify to its good effects. The programme commonly includes writing a gratitude list every evening, noting 10 things from the day for which to be grateful. Gratitude is often reported by AA members as helping them to make a connection with their Higher Power.

Carl said he felt that connection when he was grateful for the sea, the mountains, or while running. Nature reminded him of the time he had experienced a shift from agnosticism to faith in God. During our interview, just talking about it moved him to the point of making him weep. Having adopted a completely new attitude, he considered both the past and present as assets that kept him in recovery.

"I am grateful for the Higher Power's protection from negative thinking, which is part of the addictive disease. Remembering the past gives me overwhelming gratitude to the HP for the present."

Gratitude might open the door to spirituality for atheists or agnostics who find difficult to accept the very idea of faith in a higher power. This was Annie's case. As she had remained sober by following the 12 Steps to the best of her ability, she became grateful for her life and was able to report that she had obtained the promise of 'a life beyond her wildest dreams'.

People describe a ripple effect from practising gratitude. Hence, they talk about spontaneously feeling grateful because of *working* the AA programme. John had viewed himself through the negative lens of alcoholism. He saw his new feelings of gratitude as evidence that he had truly gone through a shift.

"One of the things that I try to do is a gratitude list, which I share with other people."

He envisioned prayer and gratitude as reminders for sobriety. By practising those new habits, he was conditioning himself to have new positive responses and deconditioning himself to his old negative ones.

"I thought that one of the things prayer does – particularly thanking God for a sober day and asking for another sober day – is that it reinforces your awareness that you have an addiction problem, and it keeps it in mind. And if you're praying on a daily basis for a sober day and giving thanks for having a sober day, you're not likely to think, 'Oh, I'll just have a pint!'"

Before he came to AA, Mark had a low opinion of himself and of his abilities. Writing a gratitude list every evening helped him to change that perspective.

"At the end of my drinking, I just wanted life to end. And one of the things that I try to do is a gratitude list I share with other people... Now I'm grateful for everything really."

Confirming what research has shown, he realised that simply listing things for which to be grateful each day had fundamentally changed his view of life.[43]

---

[43] The most prominent researcher and writer about gratitude, Robert Emmons defines it as 'a felt sense of wonder, thankfulness and appreciation for life'. Quoted from *The How of Happiness*, *Sonja Lyubomirsky*, Sphere, 2012, p. 88.

Fred was grateful for having found AA and considered it a privilege. He believed that it was the power of gratitude that made it work so well. He reported that giving thanks had a positive effect on him.

"Without fail, I just say thank you for a sober day. I do that because it calms me down. There is a need to be grateful for sanity when you become sober after years of drinking. You come out the other side with some reasonable sanity... You've got to thank... something! You've got to have some gratitude for something! You could go around and thank everybody, shake them by the hand, and they would look at you like you're an idiot. So, if you can thank God, like in the Serenity Prayer, that's all right. It's a gentle way to accept it."

Although he still considered himself an atheist, he regularly prayed, meditated and wrote a gratitude list. When he felt the need to justify those practices, he compared himself to other atheists.

"I know a lot of atheists who pray. They get on their knees in the morning. They give thanks for a sober day. It's very positive. But they don't have a God... The atheists and agnostics who pray and use the word 'God', that's more phenomenal than anything else!"

PRAYER

Alex observed that AA members sometimes used set prayers, depending on the need or the situation. For example, he applied the Serenity Prayer when he did not know what to do. It helped him to distinguish between what he could and could not do on his own. He realised that there were some practical things that he could do and other things, usually more spiritual, that he could not do alone.

"Therefore, it's possible for me to do things that I couldn't otherwise do or to do the things that I would do but do them better. Sadly, that doesn't happen very often because I tend to rely on myself. But what it means is that I have a resource I can use as much as I want, and it is like a safety net. The resource is there for the things I can't do. What I have to recognise is there are certain things that I can do and certain things I can't. I don't need help with my tax return, I can do that. But I can't manage depression on my own... So, you work on the things you can change, and see what happens."

Emma applied the AA slogan *Keep it simple* to prayer. She remarked how different it was from the prayers she had learned when growing up as a Catholic. She had noticed the lack of power of "vain repetitions"[44] and questioned the sincerity of her own prayers.

"Sometimes, I struggle with the prayers because again of my upbringing. There's a lot of saying of prayers and not really thinking about what they mean, and that's still a habit."

She refrained from asking for things in prayer and instead prayed for help *through* what she experienced.

"I'm careful not to pray for stuff because that's taking back my self-will. And my self-will doesn't get me anywhere. I don't pray for things to get better, but I pray to get through something. I pray, 'Oh, let me do the best I can! Just be with me! Give me guidance'... I have ten little marbles, and in the morning, I put them out, one for each thing I'm worried about. I hand that over to God. And then

---

[44] *KJV*, Matthew 6:7, "But when ye pray, use not vain repetitions, as the heathen do: for they think that they shall be heard for their much speaking.

the same marbles at the end of the day are for the things I'm grateful for. So, I'm starting my day by handing over[45] things I am scared of, and I'm finishing it with the things I'm thankful for."

MEDITATION

Research has shown that meditation modified the brain, developing new healthy neurons and getting rid of unhealthy ones. Neuroscientist Caroline Leaf wrote, "As we consciously direct our thinking, we can wire out toxic patterns of thinking and replace them with healthy thoughts. New thought networks grow."[46]

Dom regularly practised meditation. Though it did not come easily for him, it transformed his life.

"I tend to get mangled up a bit through life's events. I find it difficult to do meditation on a regular basis, not when things are going well, because if I'm doing well, I think, 'Well, what would I rather be doing? Half an hour in bed, half an hour watching TV, or half an hour sitting very still?' I'm just in a good phase now, whereas if I don't meditate for a few days, I get angry and agitated. But I've got the wisdom, which you build up after many years, to know to do it. Meditation was my only refuge from very difficult times because you can talk to people, but they don't really get what you're on about. They'll listen, but they can only help so much... When I meditate, I let my thinking go and ask the HP to come in, God's presence... You think, 'Well, I'm going

---

[45] Handing over is one of the practices AA recommends. It means sending your difficulties or burdens to the Higher Power. It parallels the Scripture, "Casting all your care upon Him; for He cares for you." *New Testament*, KJV, 1 Peter 5:7.

[46] Leaf C., *Switch on Your Brain*, Baker Books, USA, 2013, p.20.

to wake up, say, an hour early, and I'll meditate for half an hour.' Then the day takes on a different flavour. My sponsor suggested meditation. So, in terms of practical things, I do meditation most mornings, I pray quite a lot of the days... I cannot stress enough the importance of meditation! If I didn't meditate, I'd really feel the effects, and I do it on most days... I was very unhappy for my first four years in recovery, just struggling horrendously, even though it was better being non-drinking and it was nice going to meetings... This person suggested I try a type of Christian meditation. It implies saying a mantra in your head which is, 'Maranatha, come Lord Jesus' over and over for half an hour. You're supposed to do it twice a day... When I really struggle, I do that."

Meditation helped him grow out of the depression that had plagued him for a long time. It helped him feel closer to God.

"Meditation changes your life in a way you can't. You're not the same person... If you do meditation properly, you realise how damaging thoughts are! Then it might not be pleasant all day or you might still be stinging from the day before, but the day is changed. It's not like, 'Oh my God, I cannot do this!' You just get on with the day. Meditation is powerful and I do it again at the end of the day."

He changed his thinking by regularly directing it in his practice of meditation.

CHAPTER 6

Higher Power

The expression Higher Power (HP), first coined by Alcoholics Anonymous, was subsequently taken on by the different 12-Step programmes that followed. It is simply defined as "a power greater than ourselves" (Step 2).

New members are encouraged to choose for their Higher Power a power that they could consider greater than themselves, whatever it would be. However, the *AA Book* does define some specific criteria such as "loving and caring", "benevolent", or "protecting". Those do not apply to all individual choices. For example, the Universe, which some people look upon as their Higher Power, does not fulfil the Big Book's criteria. Nevertheless, the criteria can be considered as only suggested guidelines, so people do not have to follow them. AA fellows like to put newcomers at ease by telling them, "Take what you like and leave the rest."

As Alex underlined, one of the sayings that bring many to accept AA spirituality is the offer to consider God "as we understand God". Following this idea, anything can be viewed as a Higher Power as long as it is not oneself. This last condition is critical because alcoholics (and other addicts) are used to following their own will and impulses, and that is what leads them to problems.

In this large open field of choices, individuals' Higher Powers may be random characters as well as mystical representations of God. Newcomers can choose AA and its programme as a Higher Power. AA can be accepted by all its members as at least an instrument of the Higher Power.

Logically, various choices of Higher Powers will lead to various outcomes in life, but the simple fact of believing in a power higher than oneself, whatever that power may be, impacts AA members' lives positively. As Fred mentioned, its centrality in the AA programme seems to "rub off" on fellows. Consequently, in practice, they act increasingly like "believers" in their everyday lives.

It was not just the understanding of the Higher Power, but the application of the programme with its practices that affected the interviewees.

We will examine different decisions our interviewees made regarding who or what to put above themselves. They range from being far away from any concept of God to God Himself. We will also take a look at the consequences of those decisions in people's everyday lives.

HARRY POTTER

When Annie first received the suggestion to choose a Higher Power, she was very resistant. Later, when she witnessed the recovery others achieved, she decided to try. Since she did not really know how, she took on a random character that came to her mind.

"I'm completely atheist! It could be anything. It's nothing concrete for me, it has no image. It's certainly not visible. I can't come up with a mathematical formula that would say, 'A = B, therefore C must be the Higher Power'... At the time the Harry Potter film was on so, 'HP: Harry Potter'. I just thought that would do!"

Though she still could not take the question seriously, she thought that an interpretation, which superficially seemed to her as complying, would help her to gain the programme's advantages. Such a compromise might be initially okay, but it puts limits on one's recovery and probably on ultimate fulfilment in life.

ABOUT THE UNIVERSE, AA ITSELF

Some people who also had no previous spiritual beliefs tried more seriously to choose a Higher Power that could help them to become and remain sober.

John observed that some people chose the "Power of the Universe", but he realised that it did not fulfil all the criteria cited in the AA Book.

"It fails on the criteria of care and protection."

He decided his Higher Power would have to follow the criteria of benevolence. With that in mind, he chose the AA group, as had been suggested to him, over the Universe.

ANOTHER-WORLDLY LIFE FORCE

In AA, Mark finally accepted that his life had not really been fun and would never be fun if he continued to feed his addiction.

"I think that my HP has led me through the destruction alcohol has wrought to a message that says, 'Have a look at what's happened around you... Now make your decision on whether you believe you have something to contribute.' It's as simple as that: with life now moving forward like the HP has shown me, if you choose life, a further 40 years of physical life, it can only be in the pursuit of good things, things that don't harm people and don't harm yourself."

After that realisation, his lowest point became his turning point. As painful as it was, it led him to find joy in doing things he was reluctant to do.

"In trying to access the HP, we have awakenings, moments of clarity. I remember sharing in a meeting and describing my first awakening moment of clarity. I had been in AA for about 18 months. It was like someone shooting a diamond bullet into my head! Just sitting at home, I was suffering a great deal over losing someone. I had to look at myself, my part in causing the suffering, and something made me accept some of my shortcomings. It gave me a warm feeling, a vision. It's a great irony that something I didn't want to look at – I didn't want to acknowledge my shortcomings at all in life – when I did, I was rewarded with a vision, with exciting feelings! And I thought there was more to learn by looking at this stuff... It didn't show me something instantly, it just said, 'You're on the right path. It's painful, but it will be rewarded. You will be rewarded.' That gave me enough insight to weigh up the evaluation, 'Is it a good thing or is it a bad thing? Is it to be ignored or acted upon? If I act upon it, I will suffer a long time.' Because there were other things in my life I had to look at, I chose to suffer. And I've been rewarded. I can still suffer every day if I choose to suffer... The knowledge and the wisdom that my HP has given me is to say, 'Anybody can suffer every day of their life, every minute of every day.' We can think about it and we can manifest it. If we choose not to think about it – and we accept we can feel angry and sad and sorrow, remorse and guilt and shame and all of these bad things... we can feel those, but we just need to get used to accepting that these things are in life, and everybody has them. I don't need to listen in and drink and I am now okay with that. When I had that awakening, that first time, I really looked at myself and I was in a bad situation. Good feelings, almost indescribable feelings, came, which is why I described it as a diamond into my head."

Accepting to suffer was key to his progress in recovery. When he decided to follow that path, it was as if he was entering another realm. His general attitude toward life was shifted and he felt rewarded.

"That incident of that moment allowed my heart to open, my brain to open, my ears to open. Before that, I was very arrogant and very narrow-minded. It was my view of the world. I knew that wasn't right, but it was my protection. But now I want to learn more, I want to learn everything. I've always been driven by wanting to learn, so it's filled me with a sense of wonder and attention, and ambition. It's scary... It's a bit frightening because the more one can look and seek, the more power one can see that is not visible to the naked eye. And you can get a little bit afraid. I've always been an adventurous soul, so I like it like this."

He used metaphors to describe what the Higher Power was for him.

"Embracing, comforting, the HP is teaching me, almost like a therapist. The longer I don't put any addictive substances in my system, the more He rewards me with brainpower and an inner vision. My Higher Power is a life force, a benevolent, kind, embracing, comforting life force I believe that emanates from out there. It's somewhere out there in the great unknown, an unseen force, but there's absolutely no doubt that it's nice. A common view of the HP among religions is that it is other-worldly, to be reached for. That is a nice aspect because it means that we look outward, and we can become a visionary because outlook means visionary. But I think that there's a contrasting element to that, that there is an inward perspective to HP and to life in itself... There are two aspects to it, the male and the female, the alpha and the omega. And that inward HP is as hard to discover as the one out there that we cannot see and really have no visual concept of. So that's my concept of a HP, and I would also use the same contrast if I had to objectify rather than personify the HP. To simplify it, I choose to use Father-Sun, Mother-Earth, the male and the female. It's the out there and the down here under my feet... It's a bit like a chalice. It's a religious thing, but what is in there is opening, awakening, like a flower. And it is seasonal, so we can open and close... Seeking the Higher Power can be scary as one can realise more of its power. I can't generalise because it's too individual. If I had to, I would use the word a 'force', a force somewhere, here, there, unseen, that *if one seeks with altruistic intentions, one can find.* And that's all I can say, it's a force or an energy that we can access and transmit *only* if we engage our mind through thinking about helping somebody or something else. It's accessible."

He marvelled at the Higher Power's accessibility and its simultaneous links with each individual in manifestations of power and in its all-knowing aspect.

"It's accessible. Given a choice, alcoholics accept a Higher Power as long as it is benevolent. And it's so powerful and so all-knowing that, to the billions of entities trying to access it or to shy away from it, its response is individualistic, sensing and tailored to that particular being's needs, desires and wants."

He compared his HP to a wise friend he would go to for help in making decisions.

"It's a new friend in my life to whom I speak every day. I chat to him. I say, 'Hey!' and 'The sun's out! Hi, how are you doing?' I treat Him like a friend. It's not like some big boss that I have to be deferential to. It's like, 'Tell me what to do today!' And if the sun is not shining, I'll do something, or I'll meditate or my Mum will come and visit me today through the physical environment. But if my Father's out, I like to look up and feel Him from out there, so it affects me every day because that's where I get my positivity from, my reality check from, my focus from... The first year in sobriety, I almost never thought about it. I had to train myself. That's how I felt it. It's like being trained. Train your mind to just think about it. And that's very simple."

Being willing to be trained and to train himself determined his progress.

"Something will happen... I'll make the wrong choice this day, I will look to self-gratify in some way. I'll just want to have fun, to receive something that I consider to be pleasant. That will usually come at a cost, whether financial or emotional. So, I'm into a bartering, devil-bartering situation. Tit-for-tat. But if I welcome my new benevolent force in my life every morning, then I don't go into that. I somehow ask Him who He wants me to help out there. I show Him, 'This is my outlined plan for today', three or four steps or objectives I have that day... 'I'm going to go and do these, but You know I'm happy if You want me to go somewhere else... You know I've got to get these done, but I'm happy to be guided by You.' That's the kind of chat that I have. I just say, 'Let me know if You want me to do anything else.' And sometimes, when I get lost in just doing physical things in the day, when I come back at night, I just do a little review of the things I was going to do. Did my plan match up to what happened during the day? Sometimes it does, sometimes it doesn't. And I get pleasure from things that happened, 'Oh, I went out and did that!' But now I can evaluate, 'Is it going to distract me from helping somebody? Or am I going to help somebody?' I can prioritise better. So, a good criterion of a good message I thought is, 'Will I be helpful and useful as a human being?' And if there is something that will drag you off... I'm interested in everything and everyone, so I'm very easily distracted. I was as a child, and I still can be. I can very easily go out with six objectives and not do any of them. So, discipline is a good thing for me. Now I can know when not to get distracted by self-gratifying things. That's what I call wisdom."

He believed he could communicate not only with his Higher Power but also with his departed loved ones and occasionally even through living relatives.

"I'm intrigued by the way the HP communicates. But I've had too many incidents in my first years in recovery where huge, strange things have happened that are unexplained. So, two years ago, I lost my father and my brother, whom I loved dearly, to this illness. My brother was a very bright man. He worked for NATO. He was a politician, diplomat and a beautiful, gentle, lovely soul, but he couldn't stop drinking... I previously treated death like I would treat something I'd lost. I'd just forget about it and never think of it. And in sobriety, I can do that: facing pain and loss and emotion. My HP is also my lost ancestors, whom I can access and feel. When I talk to my HP like a friend, I can also talk to my lost loved ones like a friend... and through their children too, meeting my brother's sons, my nephews."

He thought there was a spiritual continuity in a family that went down generations and could help him to accept his emotions (the school of Family Systems Therapy[47] is based on that theory).

"I'm very close to my nephew. He's 27. I feel I can talk to my brother through him..."

While relating this story, Mark was so moved that he started to weep. That took him by surprise.

"I wasn't expecting that... I quite like crying now. I don't do it often, but I don't mind. This is what I was scared of previously, and I choose to cry every morning. But I don't worry about talking about it. That's how I deal with things. It was always quite frightening, but I understand it. Lots of people I'm very close to understand. It's okay."

CONSCIENCE AS HIGHER POWER

Believing with the mind is different from believing with the heart. Believing in God does not prevent hardness of the heart. On the other hand, people may have a tender heart without believing in God. A tender heart generally tends to go with what is often referred to as "having a conscience". A famous quote attributed to Swedish theologian Emanuel Swedenborg (1688-1772) says, "Conscience is God's presence in man". It has also

---

[47] The school of Family System Therapy views problems and conflicts as linked to continuity in families. It was developed by German priest and missionary Bert Hellinger and described in 'Family Constellations, A Practical Guide to Uncovering the Origins of Family Conflict', by Joy Manné, North Atlantic Books, Berkeley, California, 2005.

been said of conscience, "We are all born with a built-in alarm that alerts us when we do wrong."[48]

Fred's idea of the HP was a combination of 'the power in the rooms', as many acknowledged, and of his conscience. Thanks to his progress in the AA Programme, he enjoyed being able to choose his actions instead of being driven by triggers.

His Higher Power helped him by slowing him down, commenting on his decisions, keeping him in check or telling him when it was appropriate to apologise. He used vivid analogies to describe his conscience.

"It's *having God on your shoulder* maybe instead of a monkey. I suppose it's also an *alter-ego* that can judge me as I go. It can be *my shadow*, so it can watch my behaviour as I'm walking down the road. That sort of humility – that I don't know the answers, or I'm willing to listen – is massive."

It was new for him to reflect on things that happened in his daily life. "More and more coincidences give confidence of being looked after."

When he was diagnosed with diabetes, he wondered what it might mean.

"Right, 'This is God telling me to slow down' because I was a madman doing all this work everywhere... This is turning the negative into positive. 'Fred, everything is going to be all right.' I'm just fine now!"

He was able to respond peacefully to situations that used to drive him to drink.

"If you're on the tube[49] and someone's trodden on your foot, there's a child screaming in your ear, and you

---

[48] About Step 5, *Freedom through Confession, Life Recovery Bible*, p. 1433. It goes on to say, "God holds everyone accountable: They demonstrate God's law is written in their hearts, for their conscience and thoughts either accuse them or tell them they are doing right." (Romans 2:15).
[49] London Underground.

got someone's armpit in your face ... Coping, it's coping. It's actually, 'Right, I can do something about this!' It's recognising that *humility saves lives,* just that realisation that *you* are the problem rather than they are... If you smile at people or are generally polite, it goes a long way... I used to do this as a tactic to get what I wanted... And it's just not really on!"

HOW COULD SHE BUILD A RELATIONSHIP WITH SOMETHING AS VAGUE AS LOVE?

Lily reflected on her Catholic education.

"There's so much dogma that I'm not interested in at all, but the teachings of Jesus... there's nothing I can find better! It's a warm, fatherly, personal, human saviour, comforting, very nice!"

Familiar with Buddhist retreats, she was well-practised in meditation. She enjoyed it but saw some inconsistencies in the Buddhist teachings. She observed that though it did not include God, it implied making requests, which she understood as actual prayers.

"The Buddhists say there is no God, but then they're all praying to some manifestation, one of their beings, for protection or to be well – that's prayer! Though some Buddhists don't recognise that they pray, asking for happiness, protection, etc., is actually a form of prayer... To me, when everyone says the same phrase together and is asking for something, 'May I be well, may I be happy, may I be free from suffering and may I make progress', that is what you're desiring... I've been doing meditation for about ten years now and I know there's some awareness beyond my thoughts and beyond my feelings, which is connected to the Higher Power. I can feel that, because it's peace and joy and all those things, which are described traditionally... I've been trying to reconcile what they mean by emptiness because I like it, but then, if you're told, *'There's nothing, no God'*, it can seem cold and fearful."

Pulled between Christianity and Buddhism, she attended both church and Buddhist retreats. She felt uncomfortable between the two though.

"Am I going to be a Christian, a Buddhist? What am I going to be? I need to follow something."

She did not doubt the existence of a Higher Power, which she believed was a key to recovery from addiction but wondered how she could build a relationship with it.

"That has effect, it's real. It's very complex. I can't control it. I can try to access it and decide to act in line with it. I'm quite interested in going a little bit deeper. I realise the Higher Power is central to AA... I need to work on it."

She tried to understand it, hoping she would be able to relate to it.

"I know people who feel held. They have a sort of personal God, a personal Higher Power. They say they feel loved by their Higher Power. Those people talk about their strong connection, and I'm thinking, 'I know I've healed. I've got my tools, but they've got this relationship! What's that? I just have to accept I don't have that and I'd have to work for it. The programme encourages a relationship with the Higher Power.' I'm trying to... If you say the Higher Power is love, how do you build a relationship with something that is so vague? It's only through experience that I have an understanding of it. It's not intellectual... Rather than accepting, 'it's just love, it's out there, it's cosmic', I seem to need some kind of figure, something that can relate to me as a human being."

She was still seeking while trying to practise Buddhism and Catholicism. She kept hopeful, knowing that she had progressed in sobriety.

"Cognitively, I haven't moved that far, but emotionally and spiritually, I feel more connected, and I might have more of what they call the promises. I feel more peace, more joy, more compassion toward other people, more compassion toward myself, a bit more patient, a bit more self-aware. God is love. It is good, it will overcome the bad. It can influence people. I know it kind of does. I'm not that closed to it."

A MYSTERY, UNIVERSAL LAWS

For Alex, the power felt in AA was a mystery. He acknowledged it but could not explain it.

"I don't know that I have an understanding of what the Higher Power is. If part of AA was explaining God to newcomers, I would be stuck. And one of the things I like about AA is that you don't need to define or understand it, you just have to believe it. It's good to not have to define it. I observed that, with time, AA people seem to need less and less to understand God. You know what it says in the literature, 'The important thing is that you know it's not you'... I grew up with the idea of sort of an old man in the sky. I don't believe it's an old man in the sky anymore."

He linked the Higher Power to the universality of moral laws that AA included.

"I think there are certain universal laws, 'What goes around comes around.' 'If you do the right thing, you'll be okay.' And if you don't do the right thing, there'll be internal consequences even if there aren't external consequences. I also believe the Promises[50] and that if you work the Steps, they will come true. I've no idea why. I don't know what makes that happen. So, there must be universal laws! Perhaps we don't understand them very well."

In the past, he had been unable to apply his religious beliefs as solutions to his daily struggles with alcoholism. His faith did not change his circumstances then. That used to confuse him.

"I suppose I believed in the principles of Christianity... I was very confused about why, if I believed them, I behaved the way I did. I didn't understand that."

The AA suggestion of choosing one's own Higher Power freed him from that confusion.

"I was brought up as a Catholic and went to Catholic church. I just recently stopped going... I think the AA concept of the HP is just the most extraordinary development in modern life because if it depended on God, it wouldn't have bothered me, but it would bother lots of people. If I'd had to sign up to believing in God or Buddha or Muhammad, or whoever, I would have been fine because I had no other plans since it was the last place that I was going...."

He related to the deep crisis of faith described in St John of the Cross's book, *The Dark Night of the Soul*[51]. He had gone through a similar crisis.

"I go to the Anglican Church, but Catholics talk about 'the dark night of the soul' and losing your faith and all

[50] The promises of a better life included in the AA 'Big Book' are conditional to following the 12-Step programme "to the best of [one's] ability".

[51] Dover Thrift edition, 2003.

that kind of thing. And I can understand why people think like that. I can understand how they think they know that there's something there and then sometimes they don't and that comes and goes...."

Having spent a lot of time to try and understand his life, he appreciated the simplicity of the AA programme, which did not dwell on existential questions.

"An AA doesn't have to worry. You don't have to worry about that. You can reduce it to a *Group Of Drunks*. You can say, 'I go to meetings. I stay sober. That's it. I don't need to know more than that!' It seems to me that the longer people stay sober, the more relaxed they are about not understanding God. So, if you'd met me when I was five years sober, I would have told you all about God... There's an amazing story, one of my favourites, about a little girl who's drawing a picture very enthusiastically, and the teacher says to her, 'What are you drawing, Katie?' And she says, 'I'm drawing a picture of God.' And the teacher says, 'But nobody knows what God looks like!' And Katie says, 'They will in a minute!' So, I really like the gentle, non-judgemental approach to God in AA."

When presented with a choice between an imaginary Higher Power and a 'God of your understanding' while being given time to 'come to believe', people are more likely to open up to spirituality. That choice may not only help those who had no faith before AA but also liberate some, like Alex or Dom, from the guilt that had been associated with their past religiosity. They might be set free from perfectionism with its accompanied feeling of shame. They will not necessarily reject their old religious rites – AA actually encourages the respect of all religions – but they will not be bound by them anymore.

A VERY PERSONAL HIGHER POWER

Liz had tried various paths to make sense of her life. When she was a child, she saw God as a judge. Despite that, she tried church in her thirties.

"But I could not feel a connection with anything. I hadn't figured out that my problem was me and the symptoms were the drugs. I wanted to be rescued in some way. Now when I think about the HP, it doesn't need to rescue me, but it's very loving and it knows what's right... *It will be all right in the end and if it's not all right, it's not the end.* I didn't think that before; I thought that it had to be all right all the time... I just thought I had found what I was looking for but was looking for it in all the wrong places, a bit like Dorothy in *The Wizard of Oz* where she'd have to look further than her own backyard... I go to church regularly, but I wouldn't class myself as a Christian, oddly enough. I enjoy the peace and tranquillity of church. I quite like some rituals. I know what will happen in that hour. We'll say the creed, and we'll do the hymns. It's an energy. And I don't know whether we all get to become part of that energy when we die. Maybe. Whether it's the people that I've loved who have gone before who are there now helping me, I don't know. But it's something... an energy."

Looking back at her time of sobriety, Liz appreciated her progress.

"In three years sober, I think my faith has been the thing that's evolved. It's probably only in the past six months that I've even looked at things having faith as being HP stuff. I'm a sceptical person... actually, not always. But I will trust the wrong things. I will be really quick to trust a human being, and yet I will test the HP stuff... the wrong way around. But the faith in it has grown stronger. I'm also less afraid to say it. I think when I first came in, even though everyone else seemed really happy to have a HP, I thought I was too cool for a HP like that... that sounds a bit weird... but now I'm not!"

She appreciated hearing about interventions from a Higher Power and acknowledged such interventions in her own life.

"I hear about people... they tried to kill themselves and then, weirdly, their sister-in-law turned up at their front door, which saved them. I hear them talk about that and I think, 'That's not coincidence!' And it happens all over the place. The fact that I have a healthy son, considering the abuse I put my body through when I was pregnant, is not luck! Opening your eyes to that, I think that's what's changed and evolved, really: being much more willing to open my eyes to that. There's still a long way to go and I'm not sure you ever reach a conclusion, but my faith is stronger, and it gets stronger all the time."

She used the words Higher Power and God inter-changeably, but when saying "God", she did not refer to the judgemental God she had heard about as a child.

She wondered about other people's concepts of a Higher Power.

"If something happens, one of us might say to another, 'HP moment!' Something extraordinary happens? We will will say, 'HP! HP!' Now I don't know whether I have sat down and talked to people about what their view of the HP is. Sometimes, when you hear a chair [52], someone is very specific about maybe they have returned to their religion, whatever their religion is, and they have

---

[52] Someone in a meeting telling their life story and how they became sober.

picked up that HP... But really weirdly, I don't know what my husband's would be at all. I think that as an adult in AA: in a recovery programme, God is all-loving, and all-compassion, and healing, but He is not the One who judges. There is no judgement, no right or wrong. There's just love really, and I think for most of us that would be the same, certainly the people I know in AA. There are millions of us."

That view of God fitted with what she had been hoping for a long time.

"My whole life, I've always hoped there was something bigger than us. So, when I was a teenager, I used to write letters to the Universe, and I always used to hope there was something bigger. My reading literature when I was younger, I was very much centred on the idea of there being a being or energy bigger than us. And I lost my way with that quite a bit. And when I came into the rooms and I saw that Higher Power, I was quite excited, like it gave me permission to believe again that there was something bigger than me... But it varies because some people who don't believe in a religion, in God, or are not spiritual, believe that the HP is in the rooms of AA, and I understand that because a lot of my recovery is because of what happens in those rooms. But at the same time, I've always been protected... I've put myself and other people, my son, especially, in appallingly dangerous situations, and we're okay."

Alcoholic women often realise when they get into recovery that there were times in their drinking days when they put themselves in serious danger. Liz believed that in those moments, she had been protected. What she used to interpret as a coincidence, she now understood as an "intervention" or a "manifestation" of the Higher Power.

She also acknowledged that she could not have kept sober by herself.

"I think that the programme works for me because of that extra element, the Higher Power. The fact that for all of these years, I haven't had a drink... It's not just down to something else, I've put in work to make it that way, but it's a miracle. Maybe there was an intervention of some sort when I stopped drinking, maybe... It's wonderful and I don't believe in coincidences anymore. I believe there are signs if you want to see them. They are there, but I have to choose not to pick up a drink. I had to on a daily basis – I still do – but at the beginning, it was harder, so I know I had to put in that work combined with help from Up Above. But it's harder on a day-to-day basis...."

She remarked that having a Higher Power in her life had kept her from being arrogant and controlling.

"It's important because it's made me humble – not always – but that, to me, is an important role. If I don't believe there is something more powerful than me, I can be arrogant and I can try to control things again. If I believe there is something bigger and more powerful than me, then I'm not really that important, and it can bring me down a little bit, which is not a bad thing... How important? I would never ask anybody else to believe in it. I pray in the mornings, but I don't know what I pray to. I think the programme works for me because of that extra element, the HP element, just to bring me down, to level me, ground me, right-size me a bit."

Although she trusted that she could ask her Higher Power for help with big decisions, she was not so readily confident when it came to smaller, everyday matters.

For example, she had been able to come to terms with a friend's suicide and accept it, but she could forget the programme and start an argument with her husband.

"On the big things, I can easily say, 'Hand it over'... The Steps should work for everything, even for my friend who committed suicide. It is as it's meant to be for all of us right now... It's 'Progress, Not Perfection'[53], so I start a row with my husband and forget that 'Actually, stand back. It's not that important. That will unfold in the bigger picture!' I can forget that, but maybe 10 minutes later, I'll remember. Something will come up and I'll go, 'Now hang on, we can do this a different way.' That's what I have: you're meant to believe it and hand it over to God... I don't really use an HP in my relationships. I do – it's funny – when there are things like, at the moment, we're trying to move house, very much HP stuff. I'm able to say, 'I'm not going to get stressed about this! It will happen if it happens. If it doesn't, it's because something bigger is meant to happen...' Very easy to do that in situations like that. Jobs? I'm applying for a course to be a psycho-therapist. If I get in... If not, it's HP stuff. I can do all that, but small, minute, day-to-day details it's forgotten about. Self-will is bigger. But it's there, and I know enough about it now."

Liz believed her HP was with her even when she forgot about it. She did her part when she remembered, but there were things she could not do for herself that got done anyway, and in them she saw the HP's hand.

"The bits I had done, I had done whole-heartedly and devoutly to make sure I have a safe recovery, but there

---

[53] One of AA slogans.

are other things, HP stuff.... My recovery wouldn't be my recovery without it."

She was learning the new skill of waiting and looking toward her Higher Power before acting.

"I suppose it's like anything that the more you practise, the less conscious it becomes. When you start speaking a second language, it's very thought-out at first, but the longer you do it, the less you have to think about it; it just comes naturally. And I suppose I'm just with my three years and almost four months sober, so it's still a learning process. Maybe, if I am blessed, in ten years from now and I am still sober, it will be more integrated."

Her perception of situations had changed rather than the situations themselves.

"I think that addiction is the disease of perception of self-worth or lack of self-worth. If you ticked boxes, I still have the same life that I had when I drank, but my perception of it now is totally different. I feel blessed... to have what I have, whereas before I didn't."

Now, when she does not get what she desires, she is able to trust and accept the situation as it is.

"We've been trying for a baby for three years now, a second child, and nothing has happened so far. And it's very easy to say, 'It's not meant to be. If we're meant to have one child, that's what we've got. We're blessed!'"

When good things happened, she saw in them the Higher Power's hand.

"There are things where I can say, 'That's a good HP moment!' I remember we were going somewhere and, two days before we left, I had a crown that fell out, and it could have fallen out two days after we had gone on holiday, and then? I remember saying, 'Well, that was a nice HP moment!'"

Since she no longer believed in coincidences, she could read a meaning in events of her life that did not depend on her. She took notice of the good things that happened along her way as she practised gratitude on the go.

"I used to say there were coincidences and now my perception is that there aren't. There are signs given to us, my first one being that book on the shelf about alcoholism rather than about anger as I was looking for. And when I went to my first meeting, I wasn't going to go in because there was no greeter and no sign on the door, and I didn't know if I was in the right place. I almost went home. Then a woman out of nowhere said, 'You look like you might be looking for the meeting!' Again, something was like conspiring. I was ready to leave, go home, buy wine, say to my husband, 'I tried, couldn't find it, so I bought some wine!' I'd probably be dead by now if I'd done that. But I didn't; there was a woman there, so there were things in place to make sure I got there. That's the HP 'cause those bits weren't me. And it feels nicer that way. Things feel more connected. I like it. I feel more connected to the universe and this whole bigger thing. And things seem to have more purpose. But it's only probably in the last six months that I really started to think about that. Before, when I did my chair, I'd 'just found a book on a shelf'. Now when I think about that, I think, *Bloody hell, if I'd gone to any other bookshop, that book might have not been there!* But I didn't know and I went into that bookshop, and I looked on that shelf, and why? Because that was what was meant to happen."

She believed that her Higher Power was very personal compared to that of established religions.

"It's funny because I think: instead of it being the unifying thing where it might be in a church or synagogue, it's a very personal thing. So, it's kind of hard to share a common ground over it. It's *my* HP, *my* relationship with something that's bigger. I feel blessed that I have an understanding of one. It can relieve stress considerably. I look at the moment at people trying to get their children into secondary school or if they've made the right choice, and in a few years, that'll be us. But in a few years, I'll be able to go, 'Whatever it is, it's okay, and it's how it's meant to be!' and I won't have that level of stress. Yes, so I feel blessed to have that."

She emphasised the fact that, of all the attributes of the Higher Power, the most commonly talked about was *love*.

"For an adult in the AA programme, God is all-loving and all-compassion and healing. That's just love, really. And I think for most of us, certainly the people I know in AA, it would be the same."

FIRST, TAKING AA AS A HIGHER POWER, THEN MORE IS REVEALED

For a while, Carl followed the advice he had received of choosing AA as a Higher Power. The first time he felt ready to accept it wholeheartedly, he was still stumbling over what he called "the God-word". Then he met someone who helped him with his dilemma.

"In my home group, he shared with me what he did when he came in. He said, 'The group can be your Higher Power.' And then it was, 'Yes! The group is my HP! AA is my HP! NA [54] loves me!' I didn't feel that at the time, but NA wanted me well. And every time I went to the group, I felt something there, a strong feeling, because, by being abstinent, clean, my feelings were strong."

During his time of extreme crisis, he practised Step 11 wholeheartedly, praying and meditating most of the time. After a while, he realised his feelings had changed. He had acquired a new mindset and he did believe in God as *the* Higher Power.

"But that didn't come easy. It's work, a long road to get to that faith. I couldn't just switch on that faith! I didn't even know what it was; what it felt like. I don't think I ever had faith in my life that things were going to be all right, that it's all going to be okay, that I'm loved... so, I sort of felt I was being looked after... [cries] It makes me feel quite emotional because I usually don't speak about my mum... So, I knew that my Higher Power was looking after me, that I wasn't on my own and that things were going to be all right. It's going to be tough, but it's going to be okay. And that's what I call faith. I felt, 'It's okay.' I wasn't alone, my HP was with me, and I'd never felt that. But that's the time that it just felt strong. I came through that experience with a stronger, deeper connection to what that power is, who my God is. He is unconditional love. And that's what my understanding is about the programme, about love. I don't intellectualise it. I don't have to complicate it."

As for many in AA, his HP was now *unconditional love*. Even people who chose to put their faith in an animal or any random character for a Higher Power did not argue

---

[54] NA is short for Narcotics Anonymous. Having suffered from both alcoholism and drug addiction, Carl attended AA and NA meetings. NA members follow the same 12-Step programme, adapted to drug addiction.

against that. Recovery has a lot to do with acceptance of love as a power greater than the self.

"I'm entitled to think what I want about my HP, what I think the programme gives individuals, or to show what it has given me. It's given me an ability to love and to like myself, which I didn't. I couldn't."

What had gone wrong in his childhood and the influence of his father's views had led him to reject the idea of God.

"I think that as a child, I wasn't shown love properly. I felt there was that big thing missing there. Drugs and substances, that stuff gave me relief or made me feel some sort of soothing."

When, for the first time in his life, Carl felt completely accepted and loved, he was able to accept and love himself. This self-love had been given to him by his loving Higher Power when he accepted Him, and self-love gave him the power to love others too.

"I didn't know how to do love because I didn't have the ability to love myself. Having that connection just helps me be more loving. *The more loving I am to myself, the more loving I am to others.* So, because my HP loves me unconditionally, I've learned to love myself. There is Something out there loving me! It is unconditional. No matter what I do, I know that this thing is going to love me! And that's where my recovery has shifted. And if people ask me, 'What is your HP?', I say, 'It is Love. It's unconditional Love.' I'm loved, you know. I'm enough. I'm okay! So that's my story. I've... peace! Now I have faith that everything is going to be okay. No matter what, it's going to be all right. I need this Power to know that it's going to be okay. When these thoughts, these negative thoughts, these automatic negative thoughts come up,

I've got this Power to say, 'No! We will live; we will walk through this. That's a fault. It's not the truth!' I know so, and I know it helps me when I'm tired or stuff gets on top of me...."

He could pinpoint the moment when he first felt his Higher Power's presence. It left him with the unforgettable impression that he was loved, which reassured him. It gave him peace and a new trust, with faith for future situations, no matter how difficult they might be. Remembering the help he had received in his desperate moment gave him confidence that he would know what to do in difficult times.

THE POWER IN THE SKY

Emma was surprised by the diversity in people's choices of a Higher Power.

"Everybody has their own. I have heard people who stick to the traditional ideas of a Higher Power; then I've heard people picking random celebrities... Some people have 'Gaia Something', like the earth. There are loads of different types, but there's no pressure to have a particular faith in the meetings I go to."

She used to have problems with the idea of God.

"There was a time when I had issues with God – not with Jesus. I thought God sounded angry, a bit bossy, not very kind...."

That issue some people have about God usually comes from bad childhood experiences with authority figures.

"Jesus sounded nice, but God... And that might relate to the term 'Father'. I don't like the 'father business', so there you go! There is still that. It's also a male thing

I don't like, but Jesus has always seemed a lot nicer. And even things like this theory that Jesus' girlfriend was Mary Magdalene, I like that idea. She was supposedly a prostitute and I like that."

She liked the girlfriend theory and contrasted it to the "father business" representation that she disliked. It opened the door for her to the idea of a tolerant Higher Power.

"He could have been an open-minded guy, and he seems nice in pictures, so that might be an option. But there were times when I couldn't even connect with an HP because I was very angry."

Like many Irish nationals, she was raised in the Catholic faith. Her experience of religion was difficult.

"There's a lot of guilt, a lot of shame. There's a lot of not-good-enough, a lot of saying of prayers and not really thinking about what they mean."

She had suffered from depression for many years. Her alcoholism had a lot to do with trying to escape the shame that she felt because of a guilt-inducing religious interpretation of who God and Jesus were.

"Catholic guilt… and whenever I was hungover, I always alternated between 'Oh God, Jesus hates me! God hates me!' and 'Jesus doesn't hate me. He just wonders why I keep hurting Him!' And I'd go just really beating myself up, really badly…"

Now, her idea of the HP was "up in the sky", which she found reassuring.

"It's specifically something up in the sky, looking out for me. And it takes away that fear because it's okay, you're looked after! It's been very useful in that it takes the weight off my shoulders. It helps me just to be in the here and now, rather than worrying about the past or the future, especially the future... For me, personally, it's a very childlike understanding. It's something that cares for me and it's not judgemental. It's not, 'You should do this, you should do that!' It's a good thing it's not connected to any religion... or it's not anti. Really, it's just something bigger than me looking out for me."

Believing that her HP had a plan for her relieved her from worry. She saw it as a guiding entity.

"This idea of what God wants you to be is very comforting. If God – HP – has a plan for us, if we listen to what the HP is telling us, we are going to be on the right track. It is reassuring to know that what is for me is not going to go past me. It's there. I just need to be aware."

She particularly liked the unconditional part of her Higher Power.

"The unconditional part is very important. The HP in AA is not like in religions, but it is individual... Maybe having a Higher Power that is forgiving helps with forgiveness as well. Maybe it helps me be more forgiving!"

She used to be judgemental, but in AA she had acquired a simpler attitude toward others and accepted them more.

"Because I've got this HP who says, *'Listen, if you're trying to be a good person and if you're not intentionally screwing people over, including yourself, then I am happy'*, it affects me in the kind of person I'm trying to be and the kind of teacher I'm trying to be – just loving and accepting of others – not with a prescriptive list of what I want them to be like, but loving them with their flaws."

During her four years in AA, she went from self-deprecation to self-love.

"Yeah, by having this new God that's unconditional and loves me, it helps me to put value on myself. It's saying that if you complain about yourself or something in your life, you're complaining about God's handiwork. You disown God, basically. And I don't want to do that because God has been good to me. So, I think more highly of myself. God made me. I'm the way I'm supposed to be."

When people tried to discuss the subject with her, she avoided getting drawn into conversations about it. She was just happy with her simple beliefs.

"Don't intellectualise it, just *Keep it simple*[55]*!* I just think that I am better off believing there is something more. And it makes it easier. If bad things happen, I believe they happen for a reason. And it may just be a spiritual band-aid that makes me feel a little bit better, but I don't care. It works!"

She felt connected by regularly reading the *Promise of a New Day*[56] and the *Daily Reflections*[57], little books that accompany the AA programme. Each one is composed of short inspirational readings for every day of the year.

"I read the *Daily Reflections* every morning and I feel like it gives me a connection with my Higher Power and how I'm going to live my day. And I pray every morning, 'God, work through me! Let me do Your will, not mine.' And that helps a lot!"

When she found herself in difficult situations, she "handed them over" to her Higher Power. Whenever she did that, she felt a connection. It reassured her and gave her faith that situations in her life would end up well.

"I woke up this morning and immediately thought, 'Hand it over. Hand it over! It'll be okay.' Literally, some

---

55 *Keep it Simple* is one of the AA slogans.

56 Casey K. and Vanceburg M., *The Promise of a New Day*, Hazelden, 1983.

57 *Daily Reflections*, Hazelden Meditations, 2018.

days I would be there, hands out, just, 'I hand it over, just turn it over to You, whatever You decide!' And that helps! It's humility also because even when you feel really bad about yourself, you're usually self-important, like, 'I'm so crap at this'. That's ego. So, taking that you're not actually that important, not in a bad way but just in a way that's easier to live with, just hand it over! It gives the right perspective of self, as even feeling bad about oneself came from self-importance... There is no guilt. It helps me to hear that I'm not in charge of everything, that rather than stressing out about major decisions like 'Oh, should I take this job? Should I live here? Should I do this or that?' just go with the good feeling and know it will all work out. It makes things a lot easier. And definitely worrying less just allows me to be more productive than getting bogged down with hypothetical situations that might never happen."

That process of handing over helped her accept things she would not otherwise have wanted to happen. It also liberated her from guilt.

"When things do go wrong, it helps to know it's not necessarily my fault. It's just the way things were meant to be."

Instead of worrying about situations she encountered, she had peace about them because of the trust she felt after handing them over.

"In relationships with others, it's just very positive also; rather than trying to control others and to control situations, I let it happen, and whatever is supposed to happen will happen. And that may not be the result you want, but that's the result that is supposed to happen."

She observed that good things happened in her life when she did her best to help others.

"And not just that: people telling just how their HP has worked for them, little incidents in the day, they're not serious, but they're just... some people might call it 'luck'. I think that even with buses coming up on time... I was running late getting here and I apologise. I need to get two buses to get here, and they were both right on time! And that is in my head, 'Oh, that is my HP now! Because I'm helping somebody out!' As I help someone, the Higher Power is helping me. I like things like that, even small things like my buses coming in or the nice day. I do relate it back to HP looking out for me. And that's very helpful, to just think that. Even on bad days, be just, 'Oh, HP is looking out for me.'"

Remembering her Higher Power through the details of her days gave her peace of mind.

DEVELOPING A RELATIONSHIP WITH GOD

Though Dom had been a Christian since childhood, he had been driven away from established religion by its intolerance. AA brought him back, not to established religion, but to faith in Jesus, whom he kept as his Higher Power.

"In AA, you're encouraged to find an HP and do spiritual things. It's taken me a while, but now I am developing a relationship with an HP of my understanding... The 12 Steps are pretty much universal. It shouldn't matter what your religion is. That's the great thing about it."

During a time of great stress at work, he found a book that helped him.

"I was really down. I dreaded work. I couldn't stand it. And then there was a book called *The Sermon on the Mount* written by a person called Fox, which is kind of

'New Thought', maybe Quakers or something, but it's a book they used in the early AA. It's very different from the Bible. It's about how things can change if you change your inside. It says, *'If you think negative thoughts, you project them.'* And reading that book helped."

Having tried to be religious in the past, he found the AA programme much simpler to practise.

"AA changed me as a person. Religion, I find too prescriptive. Going to religious services, people can be quite judgemental. What AA does is that people there have empathy."

SOME MANIFESTATIONS OF A HIGHER POWER

Interviewees described various ways in which they believed their Higher Power had been manifested.

The miracle of sobriety

Alcoholics see their own sobriety as a miracle. As much as they had tried, those interviewed knew that they could not have attained it by themselves. They had come to accept that as a fact. Therefore, one of the first spiritual manifestations of another power than theirs was "the miracle of sobriety", as Liz called it.

"There must have been a Higher Power intervention for me to stop drinking... I realise now I'm at the place of healing the mental illness part of the disease. The physical addiction, the compulsion, has been lifted."

Interventions, Signs

Interventions in people's lives, along with signs, are not or are no longer seen just as coincidences like they were in the past. However, they are usually not perceived as signs or interventions at the time they happen but only afterwards, when one reflects on them.

Liz had come to believe that randomly finding a book about alcoholism and being shown the way to a meeting by a stranger were signs of a Higher Power in her life. They were important enough for her to think that without them, she would have continued to drink and most likely died of alcoholism. They had probably saved her life.

"I used to say that there were coincidences and now my perception of that is there aren't: they are signs given to us, something like *conspiring*... Human choice is also needed. If you open your eyes, you will realise the HP is reality... There have been many interventions of the HP."

She observed that she needed to *want* to see the signs in order to notice them. She wanted it, so she was willing to open her eyes and understand those as interventions from a Higher Power.

Alex thought there must have been a foremost intervention in the creation of AA itself. He remarked that, humanly speaking, two drunks could never have wrought it by themselves.

"I don't think a couple of guys could do that, a couple of random drinkers. The chances that they would sit down in 1935 and come up with a solution to a problem that nobody had been able to solve for thousands of years and that it would be perfect, the odds of that... just not plausible. So, there must be a power greater than them."

As for himself, he figured he was alive because of an intervention from the Higher Power. At the time his life was turned around, he had not even considered altering his ways.

Not Coincidences, but Good Things

In spite of her proclaimed atheism, Annie also acknowledged those interventions.

"I've thought sometimes that there is no such thing as coincidence. What makes that possible? I don't know, but I do know that coincidences for me are more than just chance."

Fred noticed good things were happening.

"Certain things happened... coincidence maybe? I don't know, but good things seem to happen rather than bad when you're expecting bad things to happen every time. It's an alcoholic way of thinking that it's the next worse thing that's going to happen. And then it stops. And more positive things come to your mind rather than negative, and you can't put your finger on it... What is it?"

Trust in the Future

To feel trust in the future is so opposite to the worry commonly felt in the past that it is seen as a miracle. Contrary to their past fears and worries, AA members trust that whatever happens and whatever will happen is part of a plan that can only be good. Trust in the future was new for all the interviewees. Carl, for example, was surprised by the transformation of his outlook.

"I've changed and now I've got back faith that everything is going to be okay. No matter what, it's going to be all right."

With that new perspective, Liz was able to see even bad events in a positive light.

"It makes it possible to see a bad event as *what was meant to be,* knowing there is a bigger plan."

TO RETAIN

Annie did not like the idea of a Power higher than herself. Nevertheless, she took a random character, Harry Potter, as a representation of it. And despite that superficial choice, she received sobriety. Though she still saw herself as an atheist, she paradoxically acknowledged interventions.

John, like many New Age people today, first chose 'the Universe' as his Higher Power. When he realised it failed on the AA criteria of care and protection, he changed it to the AA group as a benevolent HP.

Mark called his Higher Power an unseen "life force" that was benevolent, kind, embracing and "other-worldly". He used metaphors, "...almost like a therapist... male and female... alpha and omega... Father-Sun, Mother-Earth... almost like a chalice, a flower... seasonal... a wise friend to go to for making wise decisions."

For Fred, it was a combination of "the power in the rooms" and his conscience. He saw it as an alter ego, "like having God on your shoulders rather than a monkey... turning the negative into positive."

Lily, pulled between Buddhism and Christianity, believed she needed some kind of real figure to relate to.

For Alex, the Higher Power was behind universal laws. He also observed a power in meetings that he found mysterious.

Liz thought of her Higher Power – God – as all-loving, compassionate, healing, non-judgmental and knowing what is right.

Carl first chose AA as a Higher Power. Going through a deep crisis during which he kept praying and meditating, he felt a connection with God. He called Him "Unconditional Love". That connection gave him the ability to love himself and, consequently others, as well as peace, trust and faith for the future.

Emma believed her Higher Power was "up in the sky, looking out" for her and guiding her. Because He accepted her, she was able to be more accepting of others. Remembering it throughout the day gave her peace of mind.

Dom did not take religion as his Higher Power anymore, but God Himself.

The main common understanding of the HP was love or loving, as manifested through that "something" felt in meetings. Through it, people found new meaning to life.

IN BRIEF: A Combination of Practices That Make AA Work and Personal Preferences

The AA members quoted here had tried in vain to medicate their pain by diving into alcohol-induced oblivion. They had been unable to solve their problems before coming to the Programme. In the AA fellowship, they received the *gift of sobriety*. However, if AA only offered sobriety, chances are that with time people would lose it, as do many who try it on their own. But AA has more to offer. As members keep practising its programme, they are promised a life that keeps getting better to the point of being "beyond their wildest dreams". For that to happen, AA guides towards a gentle spiritual path, a path of listening and examining one's life. It offers help and values without imposing a doctrine. It welcomes newcomers. Important aspects of it are the social and peer support and, as Duhigg noticed (see footnote 17), building new habits to replace old ones.

An apparent paradox has been observed, "Shared vulnerability -- not shared strength -- binds members together, and is believed by some to be the key to recovery in AA."[58]

---

[58] Kurtz, 1975, cited in Pearce, Rivinoja, and Koenig, *Spirituality and Health*, Duke University Medical Center, 2008, p. 198.

Vulnerability goes hand in hand with the *Gift Of Desperation*. That gift might not really be GOD, as its acronym spells, but it can be God-sent when it opens the way to the promised "life beyond your wildest dreams".

Each interviewee had their own favourite key practice or combination of practices that depended on their temperament or stage of progress they were at. That diversity illustrates the versatility of the programme.

Dom favoured meditation.

Emma liked to "hand over" her problems to her HP.

John "did plenty of meetings".

The "acceptation of the sufferings of life" worked wonders for Mark.

Carl majored in prayer and meditation.

Fred faithfully practised meditation and did service.

To help him in his life choices, Alex prayed the Serenity Prayer and co-sponsored someone who had a similar problem as a solution to his seasonal depression.

Lily used a combination of Catholic and Buddhist practices.

Liz was able to trust her Higher Power effectively, believing that He would work things out for the best in the end. In difficult situations, she would say, "If it's not all right, it's not over yet."

Annie kept *in the day* any cause of resentment.

Of course, they all did much more of the programme than their preferred practices, but they spoke of those as working best for them.

People who are stressed, anxious or depressed could benefit from working the 12 Steps and getting the equivalent of a sponsor to support them regularly, someone in whom they could safely confide and get relevant feedback. Whether or not they believe they are addicted to anything, they could practise the gratitude, prayer and meditation recommended by AA. They may, like our interviewees, find a particular key to address their difficulties and turn them into assets like Fred, who said of his support of other alcoholics, "As an alcoholic [in recovery], I have a lot to give!" That happened when he turned around to help others as advised in Step 12.

PERSONAL PREFERENCES AND CHOICES OF PRACTICES

The programme of recovery offered by AA and other 12-Step fellowships can be applied to a range of mental health problems generally not classified as addictions.

What follows are examples gleaned from the interviews.

From Chapter 4: The 12 Steps

Liz learned she needed to find a balance between accepting her powerlessness, trusting her HP, and doing work she needed to do on herself (Steps 1 to 6, and 10).

After a dream, Carl realised he did not need to reason about whether or not he should have faith. He just had to accept what the programme said, and faith would come progressively. In a desperate situation, intensive times of prayer and meditation brought him peace (Step 11).

Dom learned he could not solve his problems on his own. He needed to face his part in what had gone wrong in his life, no matter how hard it was. He found relief when he shared that with someone else. He compared this fact to the power of confession in the Catholic religion. A fundamental key to progress was to stop blaming others for any of his difficulties. Facing his defects of character, he prayed for help against them (Steps 6 and 7). He made his amends to those he had wronged, which was new for him (Steps 8 and 9). It was followed by peace of mind. He saw doing such a thing as a miraculous way of getting happiness and joy. It changed the flavour of his life, the whole way he experienced it. He observed that whereas in the past he had head knowledge, working the steps had given him heart knowledge, which he realised was much deeper.

Fred realised that when he helped others, he automatically felt better (Step 12).

Alex found that working with other people was the way to keep sober (Step 12).

From Chapter 5: Sponsors and Sponsoring, Gratitude, Prayer and Meditation

SPONSORS

Acceptance of situations and being accepted by others are strong keys to recovery.

Emma learned from her sponsor to apply "*acceptance is the answer*" to her problems.

Feeling totally accepted by someone, in that specific instance by his sponsor, helped Dom to progress in the programme.

GRATITUDE

Carl noticed he felt particularly grateful when he was in nature; it made him feel connected to his Higher Power.

Annie was grateful for her sobriety; she remarked that because of it, her new life had become "beyond her wildest dreams".

John had never really felt grateful before. He now experienced spontaneous feelings of gratitude. He believed they were the result of a shift he must have experienced in AA.

After regularly writing a gratitude list, Mark realised he had truly become grateful.

Fred's new habit of giving thanks for a sober day calmed him down.

PRAYER

Alex used the Serenity Prayer to gauge what he could and could not work on in his life.

Emma kept her prayers simple. She avoided asking for things but handed over what was on her heart to her Higher Power while expecting help, and felt she received it.

MEDITATION

Dom discovered practising regular meditation had a healing effect on his mental state.

From Chapter 7: Higher Power

John, though not a believer, chose to pray set prayers, such as St Francis' or the Step 11 prayer that asked God for help. He used those as goals, and they gave him the structure he needed.

When Mark learned to accept his bad feelings as a normal part of life, he had what he experienced as a marvellous spiritual experience. Because of his acceptance, he was filled with a sense of wonder. He saw the Higher Power as a force, which he could find when he sought it "with altruistic intentions". He talked to it as he would talk to a friend. He believed what he heard really came from it if it suggested helping someone or doing some good.

Fred sought meaning in the problems he encountered. When he was diagnosed with diabetes, he took it as a message from his conscience (his chosen Higher Power), meaning that he needed to slow down. Experiencing an uncomfortable situation on the London Underground, he accepted it with humility, whereas before, he would have become angry and been driven to drink. He realised that "humility saves lives" – his and others' too.

Lily practised Buddhist meditation and went to a Christian Church but was not completely satisfied. Because she heard people in meetings talking about their relationship with God, she believed that she needed a personal relationship with Him and was seeking it.

Alex was reassured in AA when he realised he did not have to understand God.

Liz was learning to look to her chosen Higher Power, God, before acting. She saw that she was more able to trust Him for the big things than for smaller everyday matters. Realising such mental habits is a good first step to changing them.

When Carl was deeply distressed over his mother's impending death, he found peace by intensively practising prayer and meditation. As he did this, following Step 11, it gave him a new faith that everything was going to be all right. While he felt accepted and loved, he was able to love himself at last. Because of it, he also became more loving to others.

Emma found reassuring that her "Something up in the sky" was caring for her. It helped her to live in the present rather than in regrets over the past or worries about the future. She believed her Higher Power had a plan for her. Trusting in its unconditional love was a relief for her and she did not worry as she used to. She also believed that, because she was forgiven, she was able to be more forgiving. When good things happened to her, she saw them as being sent by her Higher Power.

Albert Einstein said, "There are only two ways to live your life. One is as though nothing is a miracle. The other is as though everything is a miracle." Emma lived her life closer to the latter way.

PART TWO

FINDING JOY – MYSTICS ACCOUNTS

Introduction

After having finished my research with AA members, I still felt the excitement and curiosity of the explorer; the thought of possibly finding new gems feeds that kind of curiosity.

On several occasions, I had met some rare individuals who manifested an unusual joy. I was intrigued by them. I suspected their joy had something to do with their spirituality. I wondered if it had anything to do with their personalities or their circumstances. Were they born with a special aptitude or gift? Had they gone through a shift that resulted in such enjoyment of life? If I could get them to tell me about their lives and how they had arrived at such a desirable state, perhaps it would help me personally and I could pass on some of it to others.

Would their stories have any commonalities with those of the AA members who talked about having a "life beyond their wildest dreams"? Had they gone through anything comparable to the 12 Steps? If so, the 12-Step programme might parallel some kind of *natural* process one might go through, maybe by submitting to natural laws. AA members had mentioned universal fundamental laws that would be at the origin of their programme. The "abundant life" the Bible talked about sounded quite similar to a "life beyond dreams".

However, I knew that spirituality was elusive, "Elusive in the sense that it cannot be pinned down, spirituality slips under and soars over efforts to capture it, to fence it in with words. Centuries of thought confirm that mere words can never induce the experience of spirituality."[59]

---

[59] Kurtz and Ketcham, *The Spirituality of Imperfection*, Bantam Doubleday Dell. 2002, p.16.

Deborah

The first person I interviewed about her joy was Deborah. I had known her for several years, but as an acquaintance rather than a friend. She was the mother of adult children and had separated from her husband after years of living through a difficult marriage.

She had recently moved near where I lived, and we occasionally visited each other. Then came the shocking news that she had advanced cancer. Subsequently, she endured a course of chemotherapy, without success. When the doctors said they could do nothing more for her, she decided to try an alternative method she had heard about.

After her experience with that method, her cancer tests turned out to be negative. She was elated. However, that was short-lived as the tests came back positive. This time, she was told she did not have long left to live.

It is then that, paradoxically, she experienced a radical shift from leading an ordinary life to experiencing a life full of joy.

She had to spend her last days in an End-of-Life Care Home where I visited her a few times. I was always amazed by her obvious enjoyment of life. For her, there was no question: it was due to her relationship with God.

When I asked her, she agreed to be interviewed. I had not yet mentioned my idea of passing on her joy to readers when she started to broach the subject herself.

She did not think it was possible, expressing the elusive quality of spirituality researchers had mentioned.

"You can't really make a person, another person experience this. It's a very personal thing, I think. You can tell people about what you experience or how you feel, but it's really up to God for each person when each person is ready for it."

I realised the truth of it when I thought about the writings of known mystics like Thérèse of Lisieux[60] or Brother Laurence[61]. They had numerous readers, but did the description of their experiences alter those readers' lives? I could only reflect on my reactions to them. For me, those words were like signposts. Still, however good their 'little ways' appeared to me, I could not really follow them more than for passing moments before falling back into my old ways. Maybe I did not try enough or, more likely, I was not ready for the necessary change.

Still, even if it were only to progress in my personal search, I had to explore further. Finally, Deborah herself, still not believing her experience could be passed on, helped me to understand and be touched by what she lived. That was worth looking at, even if her influence was not as profound as I would have liked it to be. It was certainly worth the time it took us. And after all, according to Positive Psychology researchers, the experience of appreciation of beauty does change us. Positive experiences and thoughts make a positive imprint on our brain cells. As cognitive neuroscientist Caroline Leaf wrote, "Your thoughts and choices impact your physical brain

[60] See for example *With Empty Hands: The Message of St. Therese of Lisieux* by Conrad de Meester, Paperback, 2002.
[61] Brother Lawrence, *The Practice of the Presence of God*, Paperback, 2015.

and body, your mental health and your spiritual development" (see footnote 46).

The investigation of individuals who are models of joy could only make a good impact.

Before I asked her any questions, Deborah talked.

"I think there might be a little bit of a problem because I feel it's more an experience... I feel like I cannot put in a word like 'God is love'. I could talk a little bit, maybe about my relationship with God, but I couldn't say that I would define God because that would only be describing in a physical and mental way something that is not God."

She never did give a definition of God or, in AA terms, of her Higher Power. Her view was that religions attempted to humanise God and put Him into words with the objective of presenting Him as real, totally like humans.

She had lived quite a religious life as a missionary, but she no longer believed that human words could describe God.

"I guess that's what happened to a lot of philosophers or teachers. They found this God and it had nothing to do with religious teaching or religion. So that's what I feel about God now, today."

Instead, she talked about the change she had gone through and its consequences. As I had experienced during my interviews with AA members, it was like looking at the blurred mirrored reflection of something rather than straight at it.

She had been a dedicated Christian for a long time after converting from her Jewish origins, but it was only recently that she had really received the peace that the Bible talks about, "that passes all understanding"[62]. Remarkably, it happened after she had been told the cancer from which she had been in remission had come back and was now terminal.

Before her shift

She described herself as having been "religious but dissatisfied" after her conversion. For 25 years, she regularly read and memorised Bible Scriptures, but she felt she only knew *about* God. She compared it to knowing about electricity but not knowing exactly what it was. She could tell people about God, but she knew she did not have any relationship or experience *with* God. She believed that it was because she lacked such a relationship that she suffered a lot.

"I was depressed most of the time. I was worried all the time about everything. I would fall into really deep depression. All kinds of negative emotions, like jealousy or pride, even hatred – really negative emotions – were troubling me and made me emotionally suffering and unstable...."

Her expectations about marriage had led to disappointment. She had always wanted to have a good marriage and a good family, believing that if she had that, she would be happy.

"But when I had – I didn't have a good marriage – but when I had a marriage, I was pretty miserable and lonely because *another person can't really fill that vacuum.*"

She was also frustrated in her prayer life. Reflecting on it, she saw that before her shift, she had always wanted

---

[62] KJV, Epistle to Philippians 4:7.

and asked God to do things for her. "God, do this for me! And why are you not answering prayer?" And most of the time, she did not really believe that He would answer.

She used to pray with other people, but she was not doing it sincerely. She was more aware of what other people thought of her than of addressing God.

"A lot of my prayers were really a show. They would have to be *really good* prayers and people would need to *really* think that I was a prayer warrior."

She used to be judgemental and critical of people, thinking a lot of things were wrong with them. She would say to herself, "Oh, this person is so bad, so cruel, or unloving!" Now she believed that judging people or looking at the negative in people was a common negative human trait, a common mental addiction.

"I used to complain about a lot of things, about the weather or even little things in life. But saying it's bad won't make any difference; it will only *make me feel bad*. People say, 'Oh, what bad weather!' I used to say it a lot. But *bad*? The weather can't be bad! It's just the way we see it. I'm looking a bit differently at my life, at my situation now."

As a missionary in poor countries for several years, she used to worry about money and finances. And she secretly hated it.

"Being an 'outreacher' and a fundraiser was so tough!"

As part of her negative thinking, she also used to obsess about her physical appearance.

"... Even my physical body – my goodness, if I wasn't under 48kg! Oh gosh, that was a big thing for me! If I weighed 49 or 50kg, that was really a big trial... And I used to have a fear of ageing."

Her shift

Her shift started after she went into remission, which at the time, she thought was a permanent healing. It was followed by a final relapse.

While she was faced with the diagnosis of cancer, she questioned her beliefs. She suddenly realised that her life was short. Because she believed at that point that her life was going to end very soon, probably in months, she searched for the spirit world and for what would come after death.

She turned to books. She read *The Journey* by Brandon Bays[63], and decided to go through such a 'journey' herself. It involved going back into her traumatic memory, which she decided to do *"with Jesus"*.

"I felt protected and with forgiveness, totally free. It helped me to realise that I *could* be free. But the real liberation came later with some other books and people that experienced life after life, like Anita Moorjani's *Dying to be Me*[64], Eckhart Tolle[65] and also Joy Goldsmith, and Alexander's *Proof of Heaven*[66]."

She believed that those authors had helped orient her towards her shift. However, she could not point out the exact time it happened.

"I think it was a process, and there was liberation."

That liberation took more than just books or following what they said. It truly started not only after she had been cleared of cancer – about six months later – but after she received the message from the hospital saying, "Well, maybe it's nothing to worry about, but your

[63] Bays B., *The Journey*, Harper Element, 2012.

[64] Hay House UK, 2012.

[65] *The Power of Now*, Namaste Publishing, 1997.

[66] Simon and Schuster, 2012.

tumour mark is going up." That was an indication that there was cancer and that it was active. The doctors saw it as a bad sign because it was only six months after the remission had occurred. They said, "Maybe it's nothing to worry about, but we'd like you to come for a couple of tests."

Then they told her the cancer was coming back. Since this was after she had believed that it was totally healed, she went into shock, far more than when she had been originally diagnosed. She had not suspected it at all.

"The fears attacked me, all kinds, and a lot of negativity about myself, feeling suddenly all those negative things become very strong, thinking 'it's a punishment', then a kind of condemnation also, because I didn't give God all the glory. 'It's a punishment, really. You don't love Him, so He doesn't love you.' Really awful!"

It was very difficult for her to hear that she was actually in the terminal stage of cancer.

"It was very hard, devastating, for my kids also, and for my friends and people who were praying for me."

In the language of AA, that is when she hit *rock bottom*.

She realised that what she had read in books and experimented with, such as her "journey" when she had followed Brandon Bays' instructions, had not really worked as she had thought.

"I went really into the deep. What had happened with the *journey* was only a little glimpse, but I didn't *really* go 'deeper' or 'higher', or whatever they call it. Later, I realised that a lot of people go into this kind of remission. It's not really a miracle, even when people like Brandon Bays from *The Journey* say they're clear. A lot of people go through remission for years even without doing anything... But actually, even after the *journey*, I was still full of ego because there was a time after the *journey* that I was totally clear from cancer."

She saw later that she had trusted not only the "journey" but her own capability to get rid of the sickness.

"There was a time when they'd already stopped chemotherapy and they said, 'There is nothing else we can do right now, and you still have some cancer, but we'll see what happens.' And then six months later, when I went for another test, the doctors looked at me in astonishment and said, 'There is no trace of cancer, we can't see anything!' Of course, it was like a new lease on life but – sorry to say – it went into my ego... And, thinking back on it, I was even rebellious. I used to say to people, 'It didn't happen through prayer or through Jesus or anything like that. It happened because I worked through my spiritual and emotional things and basically, through that, I healed myself and I got healing'... Oh, another one that 'helped me', but not really: Louise Hay[67]. She is quite famous for 'healing yourself'. And again, I was not really totally free because once you got this ego and pride, you kind of try to push things around and to take control."

Like an alcoholic before entering the AA recovery programme, she still thought she was in charge. Following Louise Hay, Brandon Bays, and other self-help authors' views, her own self was her Higher Power. A comment in the *Life Recovery Bible* can be applied to the process she had followed. Though it is about recovery from addiction, it fits with recovery from other illnesses. "In recovery, some people say that we have the power to heal ourselves.

---

[67] You can Heal your Life, Hay House, 1984.

That false idea is fed by our own wishful thinking. We wish we had the power within ourselves to overcome our problems. This idea also assumes that recovery is a simple process. But for recovery to be successful, it must involve our entire self – our heart, our mind, our spirit, and our will – being handed to God's rule."[68]

When she was following what she now called her "ego and pride", Deborah decided to teach others what she had learned when she had 'healed herself'.

"And I remember a few people wanted to talk to me and I thought, 'I can really tell people now about emotional healing with that.' And I went into a study. I actually got a certificate in hypnotherapy and NLP and also in *The Law of Attraction*. And I felt, 'I've got to do something in my life. I've got to become a teacher or maybe write books.' I was almost obsessed, and every day became more so... And God was there all the time, but He was more like a religious thing. I still didn't have that personal link."

As in Step 1 of the Anonymous Program, she had to admit that she was powerless – not over alcohol, but over her illness – and that her life had become unmanageable. It was when she finally admitted it that her shift happened. It took her about two months to grasp and accept it.

"Then I really started... well, I can't say *working*, but kind of *letting God work* in me. This was really after the second time... The cancer came back, and the shift came."

She then made a decision, as in 'working a Step 3', to turn her will and her life over to the care of God.

---

[68] *Life Recover Bible*, 2nd Peter, Recovery Themes: *True recovery involves surrender to God.*

Consequences of her shift

She reflected on the lessons she was learning along the way. What really counted for her was what happened in her daily life.

"Now I realise it doesn't matter anymore if you have cancer, if it's come back. Even when it's time to go, it's time to go. It's more what happens every day in our lives that counts."

In a kind of inventory of her life similar to an AA 4th Step, she saw the negative feelings she had fought before, such as resentment or anger, in a new light. During her "journey", she had tried to fight her lack of forgiveness toward others. She realised why it had not worked.

"I could see that this forgiveness thing was more like a mental thing, like 'I forgive, I forgive, I forgive', but it was not a real thing. It still had a hold on me, and I was trying hard to fight it. Now I think that anything you fight will actually be strengthened. By fighting it, we give it power. I realised that if you accept, 'I feel angry... Okay, I feel angry', suddenly it will kind of subside, and it wouldn't have any power anymore. I observed these thoughts of being angry with people who had maybe hurt me in the past, and I would see that actually, it doesn't exist, it's only a thought. It's only in my mind. That helped me."

As working on Step 11, "seeking through prayer... to improve [her] conscious contact with God", she understood better what prayer was, what it meant, and she reacted to it nearly ecstatically.

"Oh God, that's wonderful! I mean, You know what's best!"

She believed she was lucky because God was not finished with her.

"… But not in a negative way: it was almost as if the cancer hadn't come back, I would probably have stayed a newborn baby and nothing else would happen, but it did, so God knew that that was the best."

For the first time, she was experiencing God in a very personal way. He was right there with her. Consequently, praying became simply acknowledging God.

"I realise that it's a very personal thing and maybe many people can't relate to it, but I feel that He is always answering, and He is right there because He is closer than breath. He knows what's best and He is in control. It makes me feel – not that I don't have to pray but – that all I have to do is acknowledge His love and that He is in control and He knows what's best, instead of demanding God to do this for me and to do that for me."

That is similar to the second part of Step 11: "praying only for knowledge of His will for us and the power to carry that out." Prayer was not the endless request list that it used to be. She stopped worrying.

"I just need to acknowledge the Lord's love. I think that real prayer is *extreme praise*, just keep praising and thanking God for whatever is. If He is in control, then I really have nothing to worry about… Somewhere I read that there are so many things we don't pray for that happen all the time as if we plant a seed, and we maybe pray for it, but we don't do anything to make it grow and then it grows into a tree and then it's fruit. And it's God; it's totally God's doing. Then we know it happens, but it is God's doing. And we never pray, but we know that the sun will rise tomorrow or that the stars will be there, or the moon will be there. There are so many things that are… naturally there."

Her set of beliefs, which were quite religious before,

had changed. She had become free from fear.

"That's one of the things that really changed in me. Because once I realised that God was real in me, it meant that I had nothing to fear. There is no fear in God, '...No fear in love'[69]. I have nothing to worry about. Like 'Take no thoughts for tomorrow'[70] or 'Look at the lilies of the field, they toil not'[71]. Things like that suddenly became real to me. I believe God is in control of our lives, which we know, but also of every situation that happens. And it's all connected, even people whom we imagine we pass somehow. It's all connected, we're all connected to bring what He wants now or tomorrow or later. They're supposed to happen...."

Because of her new beliefs, her priorities and ways of looking at things also shifted. Her relationship with God had become her source of happiness. As her new priority, it brought her peace of mind.

"Things that really mattered to me before didn't matter anymore. And I realised that now I don't need anything. I don't need somebody else to make me happy. *There's a happiness that is really all a manifestation of this relationship with God.* I feel these deep manifestations of God, which are love and peace, a deep inner peace. So, there is no worry. There is no fear. That's what I would say God is for me. That's my experience."

As is written in the *Life Recovery Bible*, "...strange as it may seem at the time, surrendering to God in difficult times can be a joyful experience. If we trust that God will use our trials to further the process of healing in

---

[69] *KJV*, 1 John 4:18.
[70] *KJV*, Matthew 6:24.
[71] *KJV*, Matthew 6:28.

our life, even the tough times can become times of celebration."[72]

In Deborah's case, the healing was not physical but mental and spiritual and she had stopped worrying and even being concerned about her physical health.

She was not affected anymore by things that used to trouble her, such as bills received in the mail or the state of her finances. Her new attitude was generally one of trust. She also believed that this new attitude somehow affected the outcome of situations, including financial situations.

"I used to be negative when the post came... Now I'd think, 'There's some good news there!' And since I started doing it, there's *always* good news! Also, the worry about money and finances has gone because I know that God knows our needs before we even call, and He knows everything. He loves us and it's His pleasure to give us His Kingdom. So, there's nothing to worry about. And since then, my life became... with no real need to worry."

Appreciating life became natural for her.

"I also appreciate things more and waking up in the morning with appreciation for the day, whatever the day brings. And looking at it like, 'Oh, it's really going to be a wonderful day!' So, these are all very new things for me, and it's resulted from that shift. If the day starts with something negative, right away, I have to... still, I'm not really at that point where it comes naturally without an effort, no. I have to think, 'Well no. It's going to be a wonderful day!'"

---

[72] Note about 1 Peter 1:8-9.

All those realisations she had come to, the lessons she had learned, and her new attitude of trust were at times a bit shaky. She was not always able to actualise them.

"I suppose if I really knew all that or really believed all that, I wouldn't go through much stress and worry in my life because whatever happens is for the best. Of course, it's very difficult sometimes to accept that."

Though her happiness was not constant and at times she was affected by fear, negative emotions did not have the hold on her that they previously had, as she had become generally more tolerant of feelings and of people.

"I mean, things do come up in my human thoughts sometimes but not to the extent that they really affect me. There are things that we think about, 'Oh, it's too much!' For some people, it's cancer, for some people, it's losing their child or spouse or anything like that. Of course, there are some times when there's fear or worry about some things, where these kinds of thoughts can come, but they don't really have a hold on me and I'm able to accept things and tolerate people more, and I feel like I'm able to be more honest and stop pretending or trying to be somebody else."

She accommodated herself to difficulties.

"It's physically tiring to go through all that, but God knows what's best... I can't say that I am really where I want to be emotionally and spiritually. I think I know much less now and understand much less in some ways (laughs) than I *thought* I did before... Sometimes I still say, 'Oh, shit!' or 'I don't like this!' or 'This is really cold!' But... well, that's the way it is."

Her relationships with people had become more profound. She saw that fact as coming from God's hand, another manifestation of God's intervention in her life.

"In simple words, it's really deepened my life, my relationships with people, and the way I look at them. I think there's more compassion for people on the street, about who... you know, sometimes we kind of think, 'Oh yeah, but then they'll go and spend it on drugs!' I know... but what if it were one of my children or somebody in my family. And this is God's child! Hopefully, they will go and get something to eat with it, but really, if I look at it like God wants to live through me, then He loves everyone, everyone, and there should be the manifestation... I still have these thoughts sometimes, 'Oh, but how can this person do this?' But I'm aware of it, whereas before, no. Now, it's more like, 'Oh, this isn't me! It's just the ego!'"

She had stopped judging people automatically as she used to, believing that under their negative behaviours, there was suffering.

"When people are nasty, or just really hurtful or unloving, I believe now that they're in pain and they're suffering. I'm thinking more, I'm sorry for them, feeling more pity for them. Actually, just my concept of them didn't really mean that that's really the way a person is because God really sees the inside. And I stop judging people."

She used to worry a lot about her family, particularly about her youngest daughter, Annie, who lived with her, and more since Annie knew she had cancer. She especially worried about what her future would be after she passed away.

"I also can see that my relationships with my kids, my family or friends, totally changed."

She recounted how one of her sons, who had become wealthy, had given a large sum of money each to Annie and her elder sister, who was always struggling with how to manage her money.

"I was so happy! It was as if God were showing, 'There's nothing you need to worry about!' To me, it's like another proof of God's love, and saying, 'You don't have to worry about Annie.' And it gave me peace about everything."

Her attitude was a living illustration of the quote, "Facing death has the unbelievable power to change our priorities"[73], particularly in the way she now felt about possessions and success. She marvelled about her liberation from them.

"You know, when you're really near death, you don't think about any of these things. You don't think about money, you don't think about your possessions. You don't think about success in this world. All of these things don't matter, and it's wonderful to be able to live like that."

She observed people she was close to, her friends, particularly her Christian friends. She did not feel she could communicate with them about what she was living because, for her, it was only personal experience that could show them the real way Jesus said to live.

"I have some Christian friends who are very sincere. I know they're very sincere in their beliefs, but I look at them sometimes and I feel that they're still plagued with worry and fear and anxiety and stress, and that's totally opposite to what Jesus said. And I feel as if I can't tell them, 'Well, if you really had Jesus, you wouldn't feel like

---

[73] From Pastor Peter Tan Chi.

this' because they're not ready for it at all. They have to experience it themselves."

She observed that their prayer life was very similar to hers before she experienced her shift.

"A lot of my sincere Christian friends, I think they kind of pray, but then they don't really believe. And then when it happens, which it does because it is God's doing somehow, they say, 'Wow, it's a miracle!' – which it is, in a way... There's this verse, 'Ever learning but never coming to the knowledge of the truth'[74]. I think it's so true. Because the knowledge of the truth, which is *God is truth*, is so much above our mind or learning in books. I think some people will never in their lives actually understand this... I mean, everyone is experiencing God – but they don't know it always – when they experience love or kindness."

Dreams and interpretations of dreams

She said that she did not usually remember her dreams but that recently she had two vivid ones, which she found very strange, and which spoke to her.

Dream #1: Was she serving God?

"I had to fill in so many forms, and I remember there was this person, this young man. He said, 'So what are you doing for God?' It was because I had been so active before, witnessing, winning souls, being in the missionary field. I thought that, for God, love was measured according to what I was doing for Him. And he, the

[74] KJV, 2 Timothy 3:7.

young man, said to me, 'Are you still serving God?' I said, 'Yeah, I am!' And he said, 'Yeah, but you're not doing anything, so what are you doing for God?' I said, 'Well...' and I tried to explain how I feel about things. Then I woke up. And I was shocked!"

Puzzled by that dream, she prayed, expecting God to speak to her. She explained how she prayed by creating a void in her mind and expecting God to speak to her.

"I thought, 'What's happening?' So, I prayed and thought about it and God. I thought about it in a way that I sort of emptied everything and let God just speak to me in whatever the voice, and He said, 'I love you unconditionally. I don't love you less or more because you're doing this or that. I love you because you're Mine.' He was saying, 'Because you are. I just want you to acknowledge Me and to accept My love in your life, and it will manifest somehow.' "

She wondered how it could 'manifest' and remembered that it had already, just in the fact that she had such peace of mind. She realised that with people she met, just being happy was actually the greatest witness she could offer. People she saw reacted to her presence. They included her Christian friends, a creative writing group she attended, and even her children.

"Then I started to think about this group of Christian friends I have. I have quite a few friends there. And they always say – I don't know what they mean, but – they always tell me what encouragement and faith-building I am to them – and just by being happy! So, I was thinking about it. For them, it's a manifestation of God. And I thought about the creative writing group that we have – most of the people there are not actually believers – and how they say, 'Oh, you seem to always have this peace and happiness about you.' I say, 'Yeah, because I get my peace from God, not from the world.' And when I thought about it, I thought, 'That is just what I am doing for God: just acknowledging Him and just being.' For my kids, too, because they realise that I have this peace too, this amazing peace and they know that I hardly ever get upset, really. For them, it's quite a thing! So, this dream made me think about these kinds of things."

Dream #2

"I'm still not quite sure what it means. I was living in a bigger house than what I am living in, with another couple of people, and maybe I was married, but I can't remember. It wasn't clear. One morning in my dream, I heard some children outside, and it was a little cold, and I looked and there were three kids. The youngest was maybe about a year and a half, a toddler, and the oldest was maybe about six. I looked at them, and they had a kitten, and they were just standing there by my door. And there were no adults, nobody. And I went down, and I said, 'Hi! Where are your parents?' And they said, 'Oh, they dropped us here with the car and they just left us!' And in my dream, I was so angry with the parents! I thought, 'How can they leave a toddler and these kids at my door?' But then I thought, 'Well, I better take them in! There's no way I can leave them out there!' And they said they were hungry. So, I said to my partner or whoever it was, 'Okay, let's make some pancakes. Go and get some milk and whatever we need for pancakes.' And they were really happy. Then I woke up."

She thought that dream was about the will of God concerning her. This time, it was more demanding than the first dream. People around her needed more than just seeing her happy. Though her joy of living was a good sample for others to see, this was closer to Step 12, which asks to help others.

"I think it was again like God wants to use us in whatever way. And *He wanted me to be open and to open my door and my life, no matter what other people, like their parents, did*... I guess there were some things there that I'm still not totally sure of, like getting angry at why the parents left them, and to accept the responsibility to be God, you know, for those kids, and not to begrudge the situation...."

She saw in that dream a practical manifestation of the presence of the divine in her. She had let those children into her life without worrying about the burden they might be or the consequences of the responsibility that it would mean. It was the choice she made when presented with it. Though it was just a dream, it showed what her choice would be in such a situation.

"I told somebody about the dream and the person said, 'You made the right decision in your dream, you could have just said, *I'm sorry, it is the parents' problem*. And you could have left them there, but you opened the door and you started to make breakfast for them, and you knew that it would mean sacrifice and work.' And yeah, I guess so... The manifestations are also more peace and just accepting, like 'The peace that passes understanding' and more compassion, I guess. And not letting things affect me. There's no fear, because "There's no fear in love"(see note 69 on page 150).

About her health

"My health is... it's annoying, and it is not pleasant, but it doesn't affect my happiness and my emotions... I have this friend. She's been in remission for almost five years or so. She had the same thing as mine. When I met her, I wanted to know what her secret was and what happened, what she did. And one thing she said is she decided not to worry about anything and to give herself and her body what she needs and to rest and to say no to people and to be able to love herself and to manifest this love to her needs and her body. And that's all she's doing and nothing else, but then, on the other hand, she is very... like she is telling me, 'Don't do this!' and 'Don't do that!' and 'You shouldn't do this!' and I was telling her that I have relatives who are coming, and which of course is not going to be totally easy and is a bit of stress. And so, getting ready for it and having people staying, all that, sometimes I get exhausted because I do things. So, she was really almost angry with me and saying, 'Oh, but you shouldn't do this, and you shouldn't do that! You should do all your things that you like', and I thought, 'Oh, maybe she's right'... and she was almost telling me, 'Oh but stay at home and rest most of the time because that's what your body needs for healing.' But I went home, and I thought maybe I should actually slow down and just do things I like, but then I realised, 'but all these things I do I really enjoy, and I like, because that's me'... I have this situation where one of my sons – they live in Israel – one of their friends was coming to London and they were supposed to have a place in a hotel, but it didn't work out. My son asked if she could stay with us for a few days until her hotel worked out. And of course, there's a little bit of work, a little bit, not much because she only slept here mostly, but then she was at a conference and came home quite late that night, almost two in the morning... But so, the friend who was telling me, 'You shouldn't do this, and you shouldn't do that', I told her that I had somebody coming and she was shocked. She said, 'Why didn't you say no to your son? Why did you put yourself through this extra stress?' I said, 'Well, I don't know, I didn't want to say no to my son 'cause I want my son to be happy.' She couldn't relate to it at all. She said, 'I would say no, I always say no to people', and I felt then later, 'No, I would feel bad. It would make me feel worse if all the little things that maybe I'll...' and then I think next time I saw her I said, 'Actually, I do exactly what I want to do, and even though it makes me exhausted that's what makes me happy and that's what's important.' She realised... It seems like she's... I was going to say she's selfish, but no, I don't think it's selfishness. It's more like she believes that to protect herself is the most important thing. Well, it's okay for her, but it's different, a bit different for me because I know, and knowing God's Word, Jesus did say that only by giving and casting your bread upon the water, you actually gain, and not thinking about it actually, because when you're casting your bread on the water, you don't know anything, you don't know that it will return to you, but it's done. But that's actually the law...."

It is also what Step 12 indicates should be a way of life.

"I think, 'What's the use of life if you can't live it?' You can live it and maybe you prolong your life, but that's not what I want, like if you're not able, actually every day, to enjoy all of these really wonderful things that are so simple and free like flowers and sky and...."

A new choice in how to live her life was just to be natural. She also had another motivation.

"Jesus said to love your neighbour as yourself, which means that you have to love yourself, to accept – not to go by other people's standards, or what they think they should be – the way you are."

TO RETAIN

About resentment

Deborah believed that fighting resentment, like fighting any negative feeling, would give it power. But accepting the feeling of anger will help it to subside. She said, "It is only a thought, only in your mind."

She found that the perception of someone did not really mean that it was really the way the person was. God saw the inside. Believing that under people's negative behaviours was suffering helped her to stop judging them and be tolerant. For example, she saw a beggar in the street as God's child whereas in the past she would have been judgmental with him.

About prayer

Prayer can simply be acknowledging God. Deborah believed He is "closer than your breath..." According to her, all that needed to be done instead of demanding God to do things for us, was to acknowledge His love and the fact that He was in control and knew what was best. So, God just wanted her to acknowledge Him and to accept His love in her life, knowing that, if she did that, it would manifest somehow.

A good way to pray was by using "extreme praise", just to praise and thank God for whatever was. If He is in control, there really is nothing to worry about. Once she realised that God was real in her, she had nothing to fear.

If the day started with something negative, right away, she thought, 'Well, no. It's going to be a wonderful day!'

She trusted that whatever happened was for the best, even though it was very difficult sometimes to accept. She also prayed by creating a void in her mind and expecting God to speak to her.

About being open

She manifested being open by opening her door and her life and not begrudging situations.

Everyone experiences God when they experience love or kindness, but they don't always know it.

Attitude – such as trust – somehow affects the outcome of situations.

Maddie

Maddie and I have been close friends for many years. I thought it was going to be difficult to interview her because of the familiarity between us, which is generally seen as an obstacle to objectivity. However, I believed, like others who knew her well, that she had a special link with her Higher Power and I was interested in researching it. At first, she resisted talking about it. Finally, our friendship probably helped her to open up.

Despite being in constant pain from the chronic illness of fibromyalgia, she always appeared to glow with joy.

To deal with her physical ordeal, she used a simple strategy, "I don't think about it."

She had already told me that she floated above it. I said I wanted to learn from her. She doubted that I could.

"It is so very personal that the only person you can really learn from is God Himself."

I asked her how she understood God or her Higher Power.

"I don't understand It. It is here, that's all. It's here in my life. It's alive. I'm not really looking for it...."

I tried to probe, to find how she knew it was there, but she first brushed the subject aside.

"Those questions don't mean anything to me."

Later, she came back to it.

"It's by faith because very often you don't know it. You don't see it. You don't feel it. Therefore, it's by faith."

Before her shift, she had gone through depression, one of the known effects of fibromyalgia.

Her shift

She had tried many ways to get healed, from traditional medicine to being prayed over. Seeing no improvement in her condition, she had come to the conclusion that healing was not for her. She then thought that she just needed to adapt to her situation.

I wanted to know how she did that.

"What helps me a lot is to live in the moment. I can't cope with thinking ahead too much. I can't."

She also had other ways to cope with chronic pain.

"One of the things that helps me a lot is that with our God, we don't need to be someone we are not. We don't need to try. We don't have to struggle. We can just be as we are and just be... open, without worrying that we are like this or not that, without condemnation. For me, I believe that it is really *like* a healing. In fact, it is even more important than physical healing because... Yes, I have suffered so much from condemnation, from being under condemnation, for being the way I was [laughs] that one day I told myself, 'No, I can't keep up.' I can't, therefore... Ah, it's really good!"

She found relief when she accepted the fact that she could not remedy her situation. That is similar to the relief AA members find in doing the first step of their programme, "We admitted we were powerless over our problems and that our lives had become unmanageable", commonly summarised as Maddie said about managing her health in, "I can't".

When she saw that she could not "keep up", she felt liberated.

"That is really, for me, more precious than a lot of things... God gives us that grace. It is a gift not to have to pretend... We don't give a damn! Yeah!"

As Deborah about having terminal cancer, Maddie did not worry about her sickness or whether she would get healed from it.

"You see, I think I have had a lot of healings. In a way, it doesn't show, but my life has been transformed by it... I always used to fight [laughs], strongly, strongly fight, always [laughs], yeah... *To quit struggling is a gift*, I think, to have that confidence that God is here, that He takes care of everything."

I was puzzled by her peace of mind. When asked about it, she described two of her dreams. Like Deborah, she believed that she had received messages in dreams.

A dream

This particular dream was very meaningful. It revealed to her not only her powerlessness but also that God was in control of her life. It was like an illustration of the first three steps of AA: Step 1, powerlessness and unmanage-ability; Step 2: coming to believe that a power greater than herself could save her (restore her to sanity); Step 3: making a decision to turn her will and her life over to the care of God as she understood Him.

"I often remember that little dream I had. First, I was in my little car... my wheel was broken. A hand came to me from above, which took my wheel. And when I woke up, I was so glad, really very happy... And a bit later, I had another little dream in which again I was in my little car. I had reclined the driver's seat and I was asleep. Suddenly I woke up. I sat up and realised that not only there was no wheel but that my car was in the middle of the city, trotting. It drove, trotted, and it avoided all the obstacles... No accident! Nothing at all! Then I start panicking because I realise this. 'Help! Help me! Protect me!' And suddenly there was a voice, a hand that was there, which told me, 'AND WHAT DO YOU THINK I WAS DOING WHILE YOU WERE ASLEEP? WHAT DO YOU THINK? COME ON!' Then with His hand, you know, His kindly hand, He told me, 'GO ON, GO BACK TO SLEEP!' You see? And it often comes back to my mind when I start panicking for something because I can't believe that it is so simple, hahaha! And I think I should look somewhere else. And it comes back to me, 'BUT WHAT ARE YOU TRYING TO DO? NO, NO, NO, LET ME, LET ME DO!' And on top of all the constant headaches, non-stop, if on top I believe that it is God's mercy that allows me to sleep like that – I don't always sleep physically, but which allows me to rest like that – because otherwise, I really don't know what I would do...."

The meaning of that dream was very reassuring to her, telling her that she was kept and sustained in any road (or any circumstance) she might find herself. Her acceptance of it manifested her acceptance of God as directing her life.

"So, I cannot even say that it is me, it's not even I who manages, who copes. I can't even say that, because it would not be true. You see, it's really not me. It's not me because, really, I do nothing... Sometimes I see that hand that often opens and which tells me, 'LET ME TAKE CARE OF EVERYTHING, DON'T WORRY!' It's a rest for me, it helps me. It is He Who helps me. It's not me. Honestly, it's not me: it is in my nature to panic, to be stressed, haha! That's why I tell you it's not me, really. It really goes against my nature. Especially since, on top of it, with this sickness, everything is enormously amplified, the least little thing sometimes. So, I feel panic coming up, up, in me. I shake for very small things – hey, things which some time ago didn't move me at all, didn't touch me in the least. That's why it's really His mercy. But there is His mercy in each life. It may come in different ways, I don't know...."

Since having gone through a shift, which, according to her, went against her nature, Maddie had been counting on that mercy to survive.

"If there were not His mercy, I don't think I would live. I don't know what would have become of me."

That mercy allowed her to live with a sickness she believed would be unbearable otherwise.

"...Even inconceivable, unbelievable. I find that His mercy is very real... For me, it would be inconceivable to live without it because I have the illness, I have the sufferings."

Her sickness and her suffering had taught her to live in the present, where she felt accepted by God.

"It is certainly since that time that my life has been completely transformed... I remember a few days after I fell. We didn't know what I had. And I remember that... I was often alone at that time because I couldn't do anything. I was at the foot of my bed praying, and I was desperate. I don't remember whether I opened my Bible and read that or if I had it in my head, but I remember very well that verse, "*I will deliver you of your evil works, of every evil works"*[75] – it shocked me! Oh, how it shocked me!"

She had been extremely dedicated, giving her all to what she thought was God's service. Therefore, she was shocked when she heard that all of her efforts had been in vain. Not only had they brought no real positive results, but they had actually been shown to her as evil.

"And that was the start of seeing myself really as I was and for me, it was, 'Oh wow!' because I was trying so much all the time, I was struggling. I was... 100%... 200% wasn't enough."

Memory of an older dream

Deeply troubled by what she accepted as a revelation, she remembered another dream she had dreamt years before.

"And there I saw a little bit – I had just a glimpse because those things often come step by step – I saw how God saw [laughs] my efforts. Oh, how it shocked me! Therefore, I knew that it was from the Lord. Yes, I knew it was from the Lord. I remembered that years before – my last son was very small – I had had a dream. I was a big monkey [laughs], yes, a big monkey... Wait, not a monkey, but a big orangutan, something like that, on a pedestal. But then, wait, the pedestal was held together by pieces of wood, and on each piece was written *SELF-RIGHTEOUSNESS, PRIDE, FALSE PRETENCE...* Ugh, you name it, written on each piece of wood that were props, lifting that [laughs] kind of pedestal which had no worth whatsoever. And suddenly a hand appeared with

---

[75] *KJV*, 2nd Timothy 4:18.

an axe which demolished everything, just like that. And I fell all the way down. And I started to grow like that. And I had beautiful long hair – I, who always dreamed of having long hair – which I never had, I had beautiful hair like that... That was the dream already, which I couldn't grasp. I had to be cut down to start to glimpse because I didn't see, didn't understand what all that meant... That was a good dream! It doesn't mean that it is always there but never mind, now at least I tell myself, 'It doesn't matter, well yes, that's how I am, so what, so what?' I mean, that's great because we're all like that, like some kind of monkey on a pedestal, you know? Yes, that is why Jesus died for us. Otherwise, He wouldn't have needed to!"

She said the pedestal she saw was held mostly by pride.

"...Really by false pretence, self-righteousness, and everything like envy, pride, stinginess, all of it!"

She was grateful to understand it.

"It does me good."

She saw it as an occasion for a cleansing.

"But the cleansing goes on non-stop. It is good when we can look at ourselves and not be too scared... [bursts out laughing] and tell ourselves, 'Ok, yes, so what? That's my nature, a mess, I am a mess, but well, it doesn't matter.' I find it a relief to be able to say that we are not worth more than anyone else. That's a big relief. It is like getting rid of the old rags, of the old disguise... You've got some stuff that looks beautiful as if you were disguised as a queen or something, but it is all old rags, nothing at all actually [laughs]."

Quitting the struggle. A glimpse of the other side

Those messages from her dreams gave her guidance for managing not only her sickness but also her attitude toward life.

"I have had a lot of little dreams which helped me. They had to be dreams because I am hard-headed, very stubborn. Even when I was unwell, sometimes I would still fight. There have been a lot of little things that happened, and it was as if my heart broke into a thousand pieces... And on the wall! I remember, at that time, I was lying in bed, and on the wall, I saw water, like a small river. And it seemed to me that I needed to be like the water and let it flow – not try to go through. It was God speaking to me, telling me not to try to go through the rocks, that it did not work. But what He does is: the water follows its current. That is what helped me to say, 'Yes, okay, I'll go there.' You see, I am pig-headed!"

Now, with her sickness, she was not stubborn. She allowed herself to be carried along by it.

"It was manifested strongly when I had that deep depression a few years ago, not to fight against it but to welcome it in my life and to live, to continue to live with the depression. That helped me a lot to continue and to remember that. I remember writing to continue that. It is the same for the physical pains: not to fight against the pains, not fight but to welcome them – it's a bit much, but to live with – because I find it much easier... I don't know how others do. Each one is different."

I asked her if there were moments when she resisted the pain instead of welcoming it.

"It happens but very, very rarely. If it happens, it doesn't last. I think, 'Oh shit!' But it doesn't last long, really, and it is very, very rare, practically, since the start of the sickness. I remember when I fell, I was practically unconscious and I was carried to bed, and it seems to me that I cried for at least three days. But those were tears of relief because everything might have fallen, and I certainly didn't care. As for me, I was in the arms of Jesus and all was well, all was perfect. So, from the start, I think I have had that peace, knowing that it was well... And after that, I remember I was in the garden hanging out the washing – I was starting to do a few things. Suddenly I had the sensation that everything was perfect, that my husband was perfect, that my children were perfect, our situation was perfect, everything, that I had nothing to change – because I used to always try to change things, to plot stuff [laughs]. I wanted to change my husband. I wanted to change my children, of course. Nothing was to my taste. And there, it was so real that I could have touched the fact that everything was perfect.

And that also helped me a lot to realise that in God, all is perfect. Of course, we are not perfect, but all is perfect anyway, all is perfect in God. And it still helps me now, even with the children, because nothing is perfect. There are still always little things you see, of course. But somehow, it's perfect. All is perfect. We also are perfect in God in spite of our props. Because there are the two sides, but with God, in His light, all is perfect. Isn't it beautiful? We are spoiled, I think, very spoiled, to have such a God Who gives us another dimension, above what we can see with the eyes of the flesh...."

I wondered if she considered her dreams, their interpretations and all that sustained her in her illness as revelations.

"Oh yes, absolutely. That is why I tell you, when you ask me, 'How do you cope?', that I can't tell you because it is not me who does it. I don't feel as if I am coping. I don't feel like I am the one who copes or I am the one who manages it. Not at all."

She felt she had received glimpses of the other side, and those glimpses upheld her.

"Yes, that's it. That's very true because I was very tired. And I didn't understand why we had to read so many books. What was the use in our life with God? I tried to read some new ones, but you see, I quickly tired of them too...."

She could only live a simple life. As King Solomon, reputed to be the wisest man on earth, said, "Of making many books there is no end; and much study is a weariness of the flesh."[76]

---

[76] KJV, Book of Ecclesiastes 12:12

TO RETAIN

Not think ahead too much but live in the moment. Live in the present and feel accepted by God.

Not worry about whether to get healed from sickness or not.

Quit struggling and have confidence that God is here and takes care of everything.

Maddie accepted she was just as she was, without condemnation.

It was a relief to be able to believe that she was not worth more than anyone else.

When in depression, she did not fight against it but welcomed it and continued to live with it; it was the same for physical pains: she did not fight against them but welcomed them.

She realised that *in God, all was perfect*. Of course, no human is perfect, but all is perfect anyway in God. God gives another dimension above what can be seen with the eyes of the flesh.

Anthony

Background

When I met Anthony in a social context, I noticed a peace about him which attracted my curiosity.

In our interview, he started by describing his childhood.

"I grew up in a Christian home. But I never really knew God myself. Everything was easy. My parents were quite well off and I didn't want for anything, basically."

He was not interested in the subject of God.

"In honesty, I didn't think He did exist, and I didn't think He didn't exist."

Then his life stopped being so easy, and he started wondering what it was really about.

"Around the age of 18, my life went a bit pear-shaped when I failed college. All of my friends succeeded, and I failed. So, my foundation, everything I'd built my life on, fell apart, and at that point, I got very lonely and a bit isolated."

He felt powerless over his life and as if he could not manage it anymore, as Step 1 of the AA programme says.

His shift

Dependent on our history and our personality, situations affect us in different ways. Situations that are traumatising for some seem easy to handle by others. The situation that was Anthony's rock bottom and became his turning point might not seem as hard as getting a diagnosis of terminal cancer or a painful chronic disease, but it was enough to start him on a deep search. In that way, it is similar to the alcoholic who turned his life around because of a simple remark a little child had made about him.

"So, I started to ask the big questions in life, 'Is there more to life? Is there something beyond me?' I went to a course about Christianity just to explore Christianity. I was invited and I remember thinking, 'I could argue'... but there was a display of Jesus nailed on a cross. No matter how many times I'd heard the Gospel before, it had never hit my heart. At that point, God revealed Himself to me and all of a sudden, God was real. And it was not only that He loved me, but also He wanted to bring salvation into my life... My heart was changed at that point."

With that insight, his life was instantly transformed. Unlike those following Step 3 of AA, he did not have to make a decision himself. It came more as a gift. However, he had made a decision to explore, which led to his shift.

The conversion he went through had the effect of reassuring him after he had lost the security of his group of friends, which he had been taking for granted.

"This friendship group, this security, that had been my foundation, the thing upon which I'd built my life, when that was taken away, I didn't have a foundation. And when I found God, I found a true foundation that I could build my life on and know that He would 'never leave me nor forsake me'[77]. He would never go away. He would never just disappear… never not be there… That gives a foundation!"

After his shift

He noticed that his thoughts and behaviours changed, particularly his relationships with people.

"Before, I would never have spoken to someone I didn't know. But a few weeks after I became a Christian, for instance, I got on a bus going to town, and I saw a homeless person. The old me would have just walked past. I would never have had any compassion or heart or hope for them. I saw a homeless person and decided to stop and speak to him, have a chat and see what was going on. I think God transforms other people as well, so when He transformed me and gave me salvation, He actually gave me hope for other people and a love. So, His love for me reflects… I think it's in Philippians 2, where you're called to be the same as Christ for everyone in the world. So, at that point, He gave me a love for everything and everyone. It's not just based on me, but it's based on me knowing Him and reflecting Him. It's a change, basically."

It is interesting to note that his attitude toward a homeless person changed, as Deborah described of her attitude. I asked him to tell me more about how his life had changed.

"I think I've always had quite a bit of calmness about me, quite a lot of peace. What is changed is: I have a joy inside me. I know there is a joy inside me because of God.

---

[77] KJV, Hebrews 23:5, "For He hath said, I will never leave thee nor forsake thee."

And I know that despite situations, there is a joy. But I also know that I don't necessarily need to *seek* happiness. I think quite often, the world thinks that happiness is what the target is, and actually, I don't think that's what life is about. I think that life is all about being in a relationship with God, and He brings joy, and amid that, you'll have happiness, you'll have sadness, you'll have all kinds of things, but there is this steadiness of joy in your heart, and you can have that in the midst of things. So, I think I hate the whole thing of seeking out happiness for myself... It's not always wrong... God wants happiness. God brings happiness, but it's not the *be-all and end-all*. It's not the thing I'm seeking out for my life, to be happy and settled and comfortable. Because I think that, again, it is putting your foundation on something that is not God, it's putting your foundation on your emotion, and your emotion is so unstable that if that is the foundation, again, that could get taken from under you."

His previous 'foundation' had not stood the test when he became unable to count on the group of friends he had been trusting. Then he sought something that he could count on.

"I know that my foundation is God, and no matter what my emotion, whether I'm happy or sad... I think there is nothing wrong with sadness sometimes. I think if you're sad sometimes, it helps you reflect on life, it helps you reflect on God, Who gave you these emotions for a purpose. God gave me these emotions for a purpose, and so if I'm feeling sad, it's because I need to reflect on something and spend time talking it through with God, and maybe that sadness will lead on again to me being happier again, actually more so in the future. So, I think

God brings joy rather than happiness. That's what I'd say."

I wondered if his views on happiness had been altered since he had this new faith in Jesus.

"I don't know if I'd have been able to reflect on that before I knew Him because I didn't do any meditation or any kind of any reflective practice. I was always quite happy. I had a happy life... And as I said, when I got to when I was 18 or 19, I went through quite a sad time, quite a hard time. And that made me seek out God. So, I guess that my emotions then did kind of rule the way that I sought things out. So yes, maybe there has been a change in me that has meant that I'm not seeking out that happiness, whereas maybe before I was."

He stopped looking for happiness when he discovered that having a meaning to his life was more important. He viewed happiness as a false, illusory goal.

A relationship with God

Asked about his practices, Anthony talked about his relationship with God.

"When Jesus taught His disciples how to pray, He said 'Father', or 'Abba' – Daddy – so it is all about a relationship with God. He is this Father who loves us and has drawn us into a relationship with Him where we're His sons and daughters. And as you would want to spend time with your father if you have a good relationship – I had a good relationship with my father, so I've known him as my provider, my carer, the person I would go to in need, the person I would go to if I had something happy to tell him; I'd go to my dad and tell him, and it's the same with God. I share my life with Him. And I know Him more because of that."

Comparing that relationship to a human one, he described what he thought was the will of God concerning it.

"God wants to be known and He wants to know us. He wants us to know Him and He wants us to spend time with Him. I would spend time daily with God. I would spend time in prayer. I would spend time meditating on His Word. I would spend time reading the Bible. Spending time with other Christians knowing about Him also helps me to know Him more and see Him at work in other lives."

He described Who God was for him.

"I guess the first point is, He's the Creator, the Maker of us. He designed us. He made everything that we see and know and do. He formed everything. He would be this powerful Creator. He's still in control of everything. And yet He is also this very loving God who draws close to us and is passionate about humans and human life. Yes, He loves His creation. God is love, that's what the Bible says, very loving. Ultimately, he loves us. He adores us."

A special relationship

When Anthony described his understanding of God, he did not seem to speak about his individual view but as giving an objective representation of the subject, even though he talked about *a personal God*.

"He is a great God. I think there's a lot to know about God. He is very big. He's very powerful, a powerful God. Actually, He is Almighty Power. He draws close to us and is very intimate with us. So, to me, He's a personal God... That's the God I know, a God Who is involved in everything we do. I firmly believe that God is a Guider. I know that God is my provider, God is my foundation."

From talking about his personal relationship with God, he expanded to the universal.

"To me personally, He's a Saviour. That's what He is, He is a Redeemer. He wants to save people from all and every walk of life. He wants to save us even when we're steeped in our badness. And He ultimately has a plan for salvation for the whole world. That's a God full of forgiveness. So that's the God I wait for – His return."

Hearing God's voice

What he talked about was not a one-way relationship with God where he would do all the talking, but a healthier two-way exchange.

"As you develop a relationship with God, you begin to recognise His voice. I began to recognise His voice. And it's not easy, but I think everyone would hear God's voice if they're thinking about things, but they just might not reflect it as God's voice. So, I would say, when thoughts come into my mind which I know are not my own thoughts, I know."

One way he thought he recognised God's voice was that it was different to what he was thinking. In some cases, it could even be the opposite.

"I remember very specifically, I'd worked for St Mungo's[78] for two years, and I decided to move shelters to a different homeless shelter. I'd worked somewhere for six months, and I'd moved. And I really hated the place I worked. And I left the job and said I'm never going to

---

[78] Charity for the homeless.

work there again. It was only a six-month placement, so I went back to my old place; and then I remember, about six months later, I cycled into work, and I'd cycle past this old shelter. And I was unsettled in my other job, so I did want to move, and I heard this thought in my head saying, *'Would you ever come back here?'* And so, all the way to my next place, which was another three or four miles, I was thinking and praying through, *Would I go back to this place?* I was looking for another job and when I got to work, there was a job email, first email I opened: a project work at this other place again. So, I had it in my heart that I would never want to go back there, but God on that journey took me to a place where I recognised this as His voice because I didn't want to get back there. I had to pray it through, and I had to talk with God through it, but then the timing of it..."

In that instance, what made him believe that it was God's voice was not only that it was contrary to his thoughts but also that something else happened – an email – which also was contrary to his previous idea. He took it as a confirmation.

"That's, I guess, how I know I would hear God's voice because I often hear something, respond to it and something happens out of it... because it is a thought that is not my own."

He saw it as a proposal that he could accept or refuse. But his main aim was to be led by God in his decisions.

"You can ignore these thoughts, and nothing would come of them, I guess, or you can learn to respond to these thoughts, and you can see God's hand at work in your life. I saw God's hand at work in my life. That's often how I do life. So, if I don't hear God direct me out of something or to something, then I struggle to leave that thing."

And he enjoyed his work.

"I value work, and the work I do, I always want it to be work that is bringing hope to other people. I know that God guides me and that I do the work I do because it honours Him, and He's directed me and changed my heart for it."

When things go wrong

He thought about situations where he believed he was where God wanted him to be, but things seemed to be going wrong.

"When I'm in the middle of something, even if it's going wrong, and I know God has spoken to me before about doing it, then there is a surety to it and then, even if everything around me looks like it's going badly, I can know that actually no, this is where God has put me, and I know His hand is on it. So even if to the natural, it looks as if it's unsuccessful, I know that's where God wants me to be."

He trusted that he should stay in the situation, however hard it was, if he had been led to it by hearing from God.

"I know that whatever is going on in my life, God is there, and He is powerful, and He knows what's happening. And actually, if I'm going through a bad time, it might work for someone else's good that God has planned."

Contrary to others who would try to avoid or escape bad situations, he was willing to take the worse along with the better, like in a marriage is "for better or for worse". He remembered a marriage from the Scriptures as an example of how to take a difficult situation.

"Spending time in the Bible, I know. I like to read things like Hosea, the book where God calls a man to marry a woman and then she is unfaithful, and God calls the man to go back to her."

In that example, God told the prophet Hosea to take back his wife, who had prostituted herself, to illustrate to the people of Israel that although they had been unfaithful to Him, He still loved them.

"She is unfaithful, and he keeps going back to her, and I think God can put calls on our lives which might not be hugely beneficial to us, or might not *feel* beneficial to us, but He has done it for other people's sake as well as my sake. So, it's not just about me. My actions affect other people, and my life affects other people as well, so I know that if I can stay firm with God in this, it will bring more people to know Him maybe... I can't really ever say that, because I'm going through this one thing, these things are going to happen, but I do know that God uses all of my life and all of it together. And yeah, I will go through hard times. I know I'll go through hard times, but I trust that God wants to save people and I believe that He'll use all of my life to do that – if I will offer it to Him."

Dealing With Negative Emotions

He believed that God had challenged him in some common situations.

"He can be quite challenging. I guess I'd see it most in my driving... You know you can suddenly get angry with somebody for no reason, and you hold on to that anger in your heart because they've really annoyed you and stressed you out. And then you can go back and spend time with God and if you've got anger and hatred or anything in your heart like that, then you will be challenged by the Word and by God personally, just because being in His presence, the presence of that Almighty Love, you can't stay the same."

Step 10 in AA asks people to do something similar, "...continued to take personal inventory, and when we were wrong, promptly admitted it." To maintain his relationship with God, he considered the anger he may feel toward someone. He felt as if he was presented with a choice of attitude.

"And if you choose to stay the same and harden your heart to God, then your relationship with God suffers, and when you try to get into that place where you're spending time with God, you can feel the distance as you would in any relationship. So again, taking it back to the analogy with the father, if you've been wronged and you're angry in your heart and you try to spend time with someone, you don't feel the joy and the love and the hope in that place. Even though it's still there and very real, it is hard to experience it because you know you've got this anger or... I say 'anger', it could be anything, all kinds of things in your heart. Because I spend time in God's presence, I can't hold anger against other people anymore. I can't hold hatred towards other people, I can't. And it's not that I was a very hating person before, it's just that in everyday life, there are these things that happen, small things, big things, which get under your skin and change the way you're thinking and acting."

Those emotions are common to everyone. He reflected upon them within the perspective of his relationship with God, as if he had personally offended Him.

"When I do have these arguments or anything like that, I find it hard to be in God's presence sometimes if

I'm holding on to them. But actually, then God highlights things so when I am spending time with Him, and often I might not even know that I've done this thing, or that I'm holding on to this thing, or this is happening, or this is affecting our relationship. God highlights it in my mind. He highlights it through reading the Word, He highlights it through speaking."

That was one of the reasons why he considered the time he spent *with* God as all-important. Another reason was his personal growth.

"As a person, emotionally and spiritually growing, the more time I spend with God, from a day-to-day basis, week-to-week basis, month-to-month basis, if I have been spending time with God, I will grow. And I can see that I become more like Him."

Growing in his imitation of God has become his main goal in life.

"So, I will become more loving, I will become kinder, I will become more compassionate, I will become more patient with people. I will have more joy. I will have more patience. I will have more assurance. So, all I'm saying is when I am not spending time with God, a few days, a few weeks, I can tell the difference within me in the way that I feel, the way that I am, the way that all these things that I am saying I do..."

He realised that he had times when he lost that relationship.

"You know, I am not always 100% assured. So, if I am not spending constant time with God, I can easily slip up in the old ways of being anxious or being worried or fearful or any of the above. But the more time I spend with God, the more time I meditate on His Word, the more I talk with Him, the more I hear His voice, and I grow. I do grow in that assurance, and I grow in that knowledge... I hope that I grow! Sometimes it's difficult to see in your own life whether you're growing or not. But I do hope that I am growing in understanding as well as in knowledge of Him, as well as knowing Him personally."

Receiving directions from God

He talked about another way of finding what the will of God is for him.

"God supplies prophets and prophecies. I believe God speaks through prophets and prophecies. God can prophesy or use people to speak into our lives and give us an understanding of His heart. For instance, when I was at university – I'd been a Christian two or three years – I was leading a CU, a Christian Union, and I remember spending time with God, and He started speaking to me about preaching. And I remember that: saying He wanted to give me the gift of preaching. At the time, I didn't really have a full understanding. I was quite a baby Christian, and I didn't really understand the outworking of things. I just knew that if I spent time with Him, He would speak to me. And that came through a longing in my heart and in Corinthians it says to long after the greater gifts of God and that was what I was reflecting on. I didn't speak to anyone about that. I didn't tell anyone that I was praying about that. And I remember one night at another CU event, someone came up to me, a girl I knew but I hadn't talked to her about it. She just said, 'I believe God is speaking to you about something that He wants to use you in.' And I was like, 'Oh? Okay.' I didn't tell her what it was afterwards. I didn't discuss it with her, and I'd just think, 'Okay, that's God speaking to me like through a prophet'!"

He felt he had a special calling.

"I still feel called to preach. I preach once in a while now, but I don't preach regularly, so am I fulfilling that yet? I don't think so. It is still something, an outworking of it is still just to trust that actually if God's called me to it, if God wants me to do it, it will happen..."

He received another direction from someone who did not know he was seeking guidance at the time.

"Similarly with taking time out to go to Cambodia, Vietnam – some of it is missionary work. Again, I was at a meeting some weeks ago. And some people who didn't know me, but wanted to pray for me, offered to pray and they mentioned me being sent on a mission and going out to the mission field. And I guess what I had heard for me personally in my quiet time, they spoke over me in a very public setting. So, it all works together."

He heard the answers he sought from various sources.

"God uses people. He uses the Bible. He talks. He puts thoughts in your head. And when I spend time with Him, He speaks to me."

Sometimes he did not want to ask for answers from people, but they spoke to him without knowing that was what he wanted to know.

"I have been given confirmations of things that I would pray about that I wouldn't want to... I'd feel embarrassed saying, 'Oh, I would want to do this', but if somebody comes and confirms it, I guess that brings in a confidence that it is what God is saying and not just me being arrogant and proud or just wanting the higher thing. It brings a confidence that God is speaking."

There were also specific times when he felt he heard clearly from God.

"I remember God speaking to me at a very specific time. I'm a mountain walker, so I go and climb mountains. I remember I was walking along a very long ridge. And it was the first time I'd worn crampons, the first time I'd walked in snow, and the clouds were all around me and I didn't know how high or how long the drops were on either side. I prayed to God, asking Him to drop the clouds so that I would see because there was fear, really. I was wondering whether I would fall. And I remember for a split minute that the clouds did leave. For a split minute, after I had prayed, the clouds left. There was blue sky and I saw the drop on either side, and I remember being more scared than when I was in the cloud, in honesty. The clouds came back, and God spoke to me at that point, saying, '*Actually, I am in control, I know your journey ahead. You don't need to see everything because if you see everything, you'll be more scared than if you see what I just let you see.*' That stays with you, these moments when God speaks to you. They're a bit out of the ordinary, but they happen in a very ordinary place."

Though logically, he was in a dangerous situation, he heard there that God was in control of his steps on the mountain, like Maddie had heard in a dream that God was in control of her car while she was asleep in it. AA members also acquire trust when they do their programme to the best of their ability. They may then receive sobriety as a gift. He, like Maddie, received more trust.

What prayer meant for him

Prayer meant first being open to receiving from God.

"Paul writes to one of the churches that you should, on all occasions, in all situations, always be praying to God basically, and I think that's what it means to me: it just means being open in anything and everything. God wants to speak to you and wants you to speak to Him. So, events do speak loudly sometimes."

To keep remembering how important God is, he felt he needed regular time with Him.

"Time with God: if you don't prioritise it, you just start to lose who God is. When I don't spend time with God, I start to lose who God is."

For him, choosing to do what God suggested meant that he was choosing an adventurous life.

"Going back to that story about returning to a workplace, I think you have a choice to just ignore that thought. I could have just ignored it and thought, 'That's stupid, I'm never going back there', or I could have taken that thought on board and thought about it and prayed about it, and I could have put myself in a place where I'm ready to hear from God by doing that. You can choose to be obedient and have an adventure in God or you can choose to ignore it and live a life where you don't experience as much of God as you could. You still know God. You just don't know the adventure that He takes you on. I love to be on a mountain, and I hear from God there. God is a person. He talks to me, and He makes me hear Him."

Practising meditation

He described his personal way of meditating: he opened himself to hearing from God.

"The way I meditate is I would read a Scripture, and I would just spend time thinking with nothing else going on around me. Generally, I do it outdoors because I like nature. And I think God often speaks to me through nature, the kind of place where I know I will hear from God. I hear from God in the outback. In the middle of nowhere, that's often where I will hear from God. And it brings me more joy as well 'cause there is a lot of joy in creation."

He would take a Scripture and do several things with it, but mostly what he calls "*chew over*" it.

"Sometimes, I also draw. I'm not a very good artist, but I would draw. I would write down the Bible verse. My meditation is just a kind of a *chewing over* of God's Word and getting to know what the Bible says 'cause I believe that is what God has sent down for us to read, for Him to speak to us through, and I know that it's living. It's alive, and when I spend time chewing over it and getting to know it, getting to know Him through it, then I know that I do grow. And I do!"

However, he did not always have enough energy for it.

"I think it is, I guess, it's not necessarily the time, but it's being able to give Him my full attention and give these practices my full attention as well. So, I know that if I am overly busy, overly stretched, then I'm not always able to reflect and meditate and chew on God's Word even if I give it the time, because I'll just fall asleep, because if I don't have the emotional or spiritual or physical energy, then I can't engage in the process of spending time. That's what I have experienced."

He did not want to separate prayer from the rest of his life.

"You can't say, 'I've done my prayer time, now I'm going to do life.' It doesn't work if God might want to speak to you at a different time than you want to speak to Him. He might want to use something in your day to speak to you about something you've prayed about. And it's God's timing. That's something I have learned. You might want to use some time in the day to pray for something you want. You want it now, but God knows the right timing and I know that if I'm speaking to Him, He's speaking to me. He knows the outworking of it, so I trust Him in the midst of the unknown."

Nevertheless, he believed it was important to take special separate time to pray.

"But if I don't spend that time, separate that time out to hear God, then I find it hard to hear Him. So, I'm saying you do have to carve time out to hear God, and it has to be separate from other things and others in life. But it's not your only time with God. That outworks the other things in life. I would say that it all has to interlink and interweave."

Helping others

Though he used to 'want' to help people, he realised that in the past, he did not really use to put it into practice.

"Since coming to know God... I think, in honesty, before, I couldn't say I wouldn't have wanted to help people, but I don't think I'd have actually activated wanting to help people."

Now he felt that he was willing and able to do something for others, which he would not have been able to do before.

"Since coming to know Jesus, I think I have developed that. I want other people to know that, and I want them to experience that love and if I am doing something that is doing that, then people will experience the love of God through me... I don't know if I'd ever be put in a place where I would have to put my life on the line for someone else, but I always hope that I would do that in a practical way if I were called to. You hear stories of people stepping in the way of people trying to... I guess I would always try to save someone if I saw them in trouble, just in a very practical way, even if it would put my life at risk as well, so I guess that is something God has put inside me..."

Finding balance

He wanted to prioritise his time with God over his time with people in general but believed he was not always able to do that. He also felt his relationship with his wife had suffered from spending too much time with other people. It had suffered from a lack of balance.

"I guess you get 'people time' and you get 'relationship time'... When I spend too much time with people, I find it harder sometimes to spend time with God because it is relationship time. So, I need to say no occasionally. I know that I need to spend time out sometimes, and that's actually part of the reason why we're going away and we're taking that time out for five months because my wife and I have been through a very busy four and a half years, a very fruitful four and a half years, but very, very busy. I know that my relationship with her is suffering, her relationship with me is suffering and our relationship with God is not as good as it should be. I know that if you spend a lot of time working at a hundred miles an hour, you have little time for anything else – let alone to reflect on God and spend time with Him."

On the other hand, he enjoyed being part of a church.

"I really value being part of a church. I know that other people hear from God. I know that when other people pray for me, quite often, I hear God's voice through them. I hear the very voice of God when other people pray for me. I hear God's voice even in conversations when people don't really know that God is using them to speak. Sometimes I can hear God's voice through what they're saying. I can see the passion of God and I can hear it through them, and that can speak from God to my heart. And God uses anyone and everyone. Even if they don't really know, He can use them to speak through them."

Similarly, AA members say that in their meetings they sometimes hear messages spoken by others that speak deeply to them.

Anthony's appreciation of being part of a congregation was also a response to the fulfilment of the human need for belonging and relating to a group.

Facing difficulties

He was able to face mistakes and difficulties with faith.

"When I'm working with people, things do go wrong. I make mistakes, they make mistakes. People don't always like what you're doing. For instance, *Christians Against Poverty*[79]: about a year after opening the Centre, there was some attack from people who didn't like the fact

---

[79] A UK charity.

that we were evangelistic. I think in a very natural world, I'd have panicked and been quite anxious, and worried, and fearful, but actually, in the midst of it, I knew again God had called me to it. So even though it was a difficult time, I reflected on it, and I just knew, 'Ok, I just need to keep doing what I need to keep doing, and if people don't like it, people don't like it! You might not agree with me, but I know in my heart this is what God has called me to do and I know this is what He wants to happen. So even if you don't like it, I'm sorry, but I need to keep going.' So, it's just this assurance, I guess, this security of knowing who I am and who God has made me to be."

And he believed that the quality of his work depended on the time he spent with God.

"When you're working with the church, you can always be busy because you always know that there is more to be done. I always know there are more people lost, more people out there who need Jesus. I want to spend my life doing that, but I know if I'm doing that all the time and not spending time, proper time, with God, then I know that stuff doesn't happen properly anyway because I'm not doing the quiet time stuff. I'm not doing the practical, I'm not helping people as effectively as I should be or could be if I had spent some time with God."

He realised that he had spent too much time working in a hard environment.

"It's a time when we need God to direct us. And I think physically we're tired, emotionally we're tired. We've given out a lot of ourselves these last four years as well so that spiritually we're tired as well, and we just need to recuperate."

On the other hand, he acknowledged that he had learned the lessons he needed to learn precisely because he was in such a hard environment.

"It was hard though, it was a very disorganised place, badly managed, but I know God had me there for a reason. It developed me and it developed my ability to manage in-depth, to manage people because I was willing to step up and take responsibility in a place where there's lots of disorganisation and lots of bad management. So, I was trained in that place to kind of ignore – not ignore, but cope with – tough things around me while trying to improve and manage."

Again, he was willing to take the 'worse' along with the 'better'.

"I think work doesn't always have to be easy. I don't long for an easy life… I do sometimes. We all do sometimes, and I do at this moment in life. I long for a bit of an easier life for a while, but with that, it's not all about living an easy life. I don't desire to just live the easy life or to just be comfortable or to be all happy myself or relaxed."

He was willing to stay in difficult places because making things better represented an adventure for him, and he wanted some adventure.

"I long for adventure, I guess. There's a pleasure knowing that in that place, I could make a difference. I could make a better place, especially for homeless people to live but also for the staff to come in, I could make it better. I could improve it. Even though it's not necessarily a happy, easy environment, there's pleasure in knowing that I can improve it, so I do learn lessons in the middle of it. I develop as a person as I learn lessons from being in those places. To walk with God, you have to be willing to be stretched. If you're willing to be stretched, then you'll grow. If you're not willing to be stretched, then you'll stay in the same place, you'll get bored, and you'll probably leave God, not that He'll leave...."

Even though he had difficulties in his work, he saw them as challenges and opportunities to grow.

About finances

He had a very trustful attitude about finances.

"I'm very lucky – my wife is the same. We would both happily sacrifice finances and money if it meant serving other people and putting them forward in a way that we believe God guides us."

Like David Livingstone, the famous missionary to Africa, he could have said, "I never made a sacrifice."

"I say I sacrifice money, but every time I've sacrificed money, money has come in. So, I can make decisions that would naturally seem unrealistic, and I've known God guides me every step of the way. He guided me to St Mungo's. He guided me to CAP [Christians Against Poverty]."

TO RETAIN

About life's goal

Life is not about seeking happiness. If it were, it would mean putting its foundation on emotions, and emotions are unstable.

There is nothing wrong with sadness sometimes. It helps to reflect on life, on God, Who gave emotions for a purpose. That sadness might lead to being happier in the future.

God brings joy rather than happiness. Happiness is a wrong goal. Having a meaningful life is more important.

Growing in the imitation of God can be the main goal of life, becoming more loving, kinder, more compassionate, more patient with people.

About Prayer

On all occasions, in all situations, always praying to God simply means being open to Him. In anything and everything, God wants to speak to people and wants people to speak to Him. God might want to use something in the day to speak about something that one has prayed about.

Nevertheless, time needs to be carved just to hear God, and it has to be separated from other things and others in life.

God wants to be known and He wants us to spend time with Him.

About Work

Work needs to be valued. Anthony always wants his work to bring hope to other people.

Choosing to do what God suggests means choosing an adventurous life.

The quality of the work done depends on the time spent with God.

Work does not always have to be easy. To walk with God, one has to be willing to be stretched. Being willing to be stretched leads to growth. Difficulties in the area of work can be considered as challenges and as opportunities to grow.

If led to a situation by hearing from God, one needs to be willing to take the worse along with the better, like in marriage, which is said to be *for better or for worse*.

About meditation

Take a Scripture and 'chew over' it.

The more time spent with God, meditating on His Word, talking with Him, hearing His voice, the more growth there will be.

God will speak to the person who spends time with Him. It comes through a longing in the heart.

One way to recognise God's voice is that it is different to what we may be thinking. In some cases, it could even be the opposite.

SMALL AFTERWORD

Although those last interviewees endured serious troubles: terminal cancer, fibromyalgia and exhaustion from a difficult job, all three could be characterised by their contentment.

AA members learn contentment step by step from the start. Step 1 teaches them that they need to stop fighting and trying to change their situation on their own or trying to control, and accept their powerlessness. Acceptance brings a taste of contentment.

While the Apostle Paul described all kinds of troubles he had endured, from being beaten with rods and stoned to being shipwrecked (KJV, 2 Corinthians 10:25) and more, he did not dwell on it for long. While in jail, soon to be put to death, he said, "I have learned in whatsoever state I am, therewith to be content" (Philippians 4:11b).

Further, he wrote a friend these words, "Godliness with contentment is great gain" (1 Timothy 6:6). AA members and mystics seem to have that *great gain* in common.

APPENDIX:

ACADEMIC VIEWS ON AA

The origins of AA

L ooking back on AA's origins sheds light on its present workings. A couple of influences, both involving spirituality, dominate: an intervention of Carl Jung, the psychoanalyst interested in spiritual matters, and the input of a Christian group known as *the Oxford group*[80].

Jung, the son of a Lutheran pastor and a spiritualist mother, had "a lifelong interest in the effect religion has on people."[81] One client he had treated for alcoholism, Rowland Hazard, came back to him after relapsing. Jung told him that, having already received the best medical treatment possible, he could not get any more, but that one thing might help relieve his desire to drink: to have a spiritual or religious experience.

Jung's refusal to take Hazard again as a patient and his advice to try religion instead marked the demise of classical medicine in the treatment of alcoholism. He had "added professional legitimacy to the transformative power of spiritual experience."[82]

Following that meeting with Jung, Hazard sought religion with the Oxford Group in Akron, Ohio. There he found sobriety. He then went out to testify to other

---

[80] *Bluhm, A. C. Verification of C. G. Jung's analysis of Rowland Hazard and the history of Alcoholics Anonymous.* History of Psychology, 9 (4), 313-324, 2006.

[81] https://www.catholicculture.org/culture/library/view.cfm?recnum=4676 Thevadasan,P. *Carl Jung's Journey from God*, Catholic Culture, 2014.

[82] White, W. L., and Kurtz, E., *Twelve Defining Moments in the History of Alcoholics Anonymous*, in M. Galanter & L. A. Kaskutas (Eds.), Recent Developments in Alcoholism 18, pp. 37-39. Springer, USA. 2008.

alcoholics about his transformed life through faith in the Christian God.

One of his converts was Ebby Thacher, who, in turn, brought the message to an old alcoholic friend of his, an agnostic named Bill Wilson. Bill W, as he is known in AA, after doubting for a while, had his own spiritual experience, which resulted in sobriety. He went on to found AA with another alcoholic, known as Bob, who had also sobered up in the Oxford Group.

'Experiential knowledge' – not professional credentials – was considered as the real expertise in AA, along with the passing on of spiritual experience[83].

The inexorable progression of alcoholism

With substance use (misuse actually), one usually starts by going from a state of anxiety or mental suffering to a state of pleasure. When those artificially created moments of relief become habitual, more and more of the substance is needed to cause the same effect. This is known as the process of habituation. "Alcohol increases the brain production of the neurotransmitter dopamine, which sends a message of pleasure's reward. Over time, the brain responds to the stimulation of alcohol by decreasing certain dopamine receptors. These receptors – known as D2 receptors – are nerve cell proteins to which the dopamine must bind to send the pleasure signal. An alcoholic will experience a reward

83 Borkman, T. Understanding self-help/mutual aid: Experiential learning in the commons. New Brunswick, N.J.: Rutgers University Press, 1999.

deficiency and compensate by drinking more to try to recapture the pleasure."[84]

Unpleasant consequences increase while pleasurable effects decrease. What started with pleasure might eventually turn into extreme mental suffering, such as paranoia or other mental health conditions worse than those that originally led a person to self-medicate with a substance.

Alcoholics may die of the disease. Some alcoholics search for treatments outside AA, with psychiatric help or pharmaceutical drugs such as *Baclofen*[85]. Many keep relapsing; they go back to their addiction after a period of clinical detoxification, to the despair of their relatives and friends.

AA members often tell of a time when they had found their feelings unbearable. They then took the path of destruction, led through irresistible cravings to the heart of suffering. The pull of the cravings can be overpowering. Yielding to short-lived relief, they fell into chaos.

Some started going to AA when they were encouraged by a relative or friend, but it is often when they reach rock bottom that alcoholics become willing to try out an AA meeting[86]. This might happen when they realise their powerlessness and become ready to try the path of recovery.

---

[84] Dowsett Johnston A., *Drink: The Intimate Relationship Between Women and Alcohol*, Harper Collins, p. 267, 2013

[85] Baclofen, since the book *The End of My Addiction* by Dr Olivier Ameisen (Hachette, 2008), has been known to stop cravings for alcohol. However, it does not stop the mental and spiritual sickness that the AA programme addresses.

[86] "It is sometimes necessary for us to hit bottom before we can begin to rebuild our life...." *Life Recovery Bible*, Deuteronomy, ch.2, note about verses 14-15.

Two Opposite Academic Views of AA

In spite of AA's qualities, a materialistic worldview has resulted in a negative interpretation among the public and the scientific community. "Current AA researchers... whose secular framework cannot easily accommodate non-scientific paradigms often parody, trivialize, or stigmatize AA."[87]

One of the academic definitions of AA is a "voluntary self-help organization". Having considered the two perspectives of AA, as a type of cult or a voluntary association, Borkman concludes that the voluntary association fits best and "is informed by the research on self-help/mutual aid."[88]

Among voluntary self-help associations, no other volunteer group can compare to it. Its particular qualities include:

- The offer of a programme for life.
- In some instances, an alternative to jail or to losing a job.
- Influence on other areas of addiction recovery (substances or behavioural addictions).
- A model in addiction treatment that sees no real competition.
- The unprecedented act of having pushed addiction medicine to recognise spirituality as an important factor in recovery. It has even been theorised that, because of that very fact, the field of addiction is ahead of the rest of western medicine.[89]

---

[87] Borkman, 2008.
[88] 2008, p.12.
[89] Miller, W. R., *It all Depends*, Addiction, 2008.

- Free follow-up for life. No other treatment organisation, whether private or governmental, can
  afford to give such continuous support.[90]

The importance attributed to the Higher Power is seen
by some as the main reason why "AA has been much
more effective than psychiatry in treating alcoholics...
because... AA addresses the spiritual needs of these
people – something that traditional psychotherapy, with
its secular humanist values, does not address."[91]

[90] Peck M.S., *Further along the way less travelled,* Simon and Schuster, London, UK, 1993.
[91] Akhtar M, Boniwell I, 2010. *Applying Positive Psychology to alcohol-misusing adolescents: A group intervention.* Groupwork 20: 6-31.

Bibliography

44 Questions, Pamphlet. New York: Alcoholics Anonymous World Services, Inc., 1990.

AACA. *Alcoholics Anonymous comes of age: A brief history of AA*. New York: Alcoholics Anonymous World Services, Inc., 1957.

Adult Children of Alcoholics, ACOA or ACA World Service Organization, 2006.

Akhtar, M., and Boniwell, I. *Applying Positive Psychology to alcohol-misusing adolescents: A group intervention*. Groupwork 20(3), pp.6-31, 2010.

Alcoholics Anonymous, Alcoholics Anonymous World Services, Inc. Reprinted with permission in Great Britain, 2007.

Alexander, E., *Proof of Heaven*, Simon and Schuster, 2012.

Ameisen, O., *The End of my Addiction*, Piatkus, 2010.

Backus, W. *The healing power of a healthy mind*. Minneapolis, Bethany House Publishers, 1997.

Bays, B., *The Journey*, Harper Element, 2012.

Bluhm, A. C. *Verification of C. G. Jung's analysis of Rowland Hazard and the history of Alcoholics Anonymous*. History of Psychology, 9 (4), 313-324, 2006.

Borkman, T., *Understanding self-help/mutual aid: Experiential learning in the commons*. New Brunswick, N.J.: Rutgers University Press, 1999.

Borkman, T., *The 12 Steps Recovery Model of AA: A Voluntary Mutual Help Association*, in M. Galanter & L. A.

Kaskutas (Eds.), Recent Developments in Alcoholism 18, pp. 9-12. Springer, USA, 2008.

Carlson, R., Stop Thinking, Start Living, Element, 2003. Carmichael, Amy. In Acceptance Lieth Peace, Word Press.

Casey, K., and Vanceburg, M., The Promise of a New Day. Hazelden Foundation, Harper San Francisco. US, 1983.

Connors, G. J., Walitzer, K. S., and Tonigan, J. S., Spiritual Change in Recovery in M. Galanter & L. A. Kaskutas (Eds.), Recent Developments in Alcoholism, 18, p. 209. Springer, US, 2008.

Cornah, D., Cheers? Understanding the Relationship Between Alcohol and Mental Health, Mental Health Foundation, 2006.

Crimson King, I talk to the Wind, In the Court of the Crimson King, 1969.

Daily Reflections, Hazelden, 2018.

Dossey, L., Healing Words. San Francisco: Harper Collins/Harper San Francisco, 1993.

Dowsett Johnston, A., Drink: The Intimate Relationship between Women and Alcohol, p. 267, 2013.

Duhigg, C., The Power of Habit, Random House. US. pp.69-70, 2012.

Farson, R., Calamity Theory of Growth, in Eger E.'s The Choice, p.229. Rider, 2017.

Flores, P.J., Group Psychotherapy with Addicted Populations Chapter 7, Group Psychotherapy, AA, and the Twelve-Step Programs, p.247-298. Haworth Press, Routledge, New York, 1997.

Frankl, Viktor, Man's Search for Meaning, Ebury Publishing, 2004.

Galanter, M., & Kaskutas, L. A., *Recent Developments in Alcoholism*. Springe, 2008.

Hawker, P., *Secret Affairs of the Soul*, Northstone, 2001,

Hay, L., *You can Heal your Life*, Hay House, 1984.

King James Version Bible, Cambridge University Press, UK, first published in 1611.

Kurtz, E., *Not God: A History of AA*. Centre City, MI: Hazelden Educational Services, 1975.

Kurtz, E., and Ketcham K., *The Spirituality of Imperfection*, Bantam Doubleday Dell, p. 4, 2002.

Kurtz, cited in Pearce, Rivinoja, and Koenig, p. 198, 1975.

Leaf, C., *Switch on Your Brain*, Baker Books, USA, 2013.

Levin, J., *Religion and health: Is there an association? Is it valid? Is it causal?* Social Science and Medicine, v.38, n.11, 1475-82, 1994.

Life Recovery Bible, Tyndale House Publishers, 1998.

Manné, J., *Family Constellations*, North Atlantic Books, USA, 2009.

Martin, R., *The Fulfillment of All Desire*, Emmaus Road Publishing, USA, 2006.

Miller, W. R., *It all Depends*, 2008.

Moorjani A., *Dying to be me*, Hay House UK, 2012.

Moos, R. H., *How and Why 12 Steps Self-Help Groups are Effective*, in M. Galanter, 2008.

Niebuhr, R., *Serenity Prayer*, 1932-1933, 2008.

Pardini, D. A., Plante, T. G., Sherman, A. and Stump, J. E., *Religious faith and spirituality in substance abuse recovery: Determining the mental health benefits.* Journal of Substance Abuse Treatment, 19 (4), 347-354, 2000.

Peck, M. S., *Further along the way less travelled*, Simon and Schuster, London, UK, 1993.

Poloma, M. M., Pendleton, B. F. *Exploring Types of Prayer and the Quality of life: A Research Note*, Review of Religious Research. (31) 1, pp. 46-53, 1989.

Poloma, M. M., Pendleton, B. F. *The effects of prayer and prayer experiences on measures of general well-being.* Journal of Psychology and Theology, 1, 71-83, 1991.

PROJECT MATCH Research Group, University of Connecticut Health Center, 1998.

Reiland, R., *Get Me Out of Here, My Recovery from Borderline Personality Disorder*, Hazelden, 2004.

Rohr, R., *Breathing Under Water*, St Anthony Messenger Press, USA, 2011.

St John of the Cross, *Dark Night of The Soul*, Dover Thrift Editions, 2003.

Taylor, S., *Out of the Darkness*, Hay House, London, UK, 2011.

Tolle, E., *The Power of Now,* Namaste Publishing, 1997.

Tonigan, J. S. *Alcoholics Anonymous outcomes and benefits.* In M. Galanter & L. A. Kaskutas, *Research on Alcoholics Anonymous and spirituality in addiction recovery* (pp. 357–372), Springer Science + Business Media, 2008.

Twelve Steps and Twelve Traditions, Alcoholics Anonymous General Service Office, York, UK. 2008.

Walker, S. R., Tonigan, J. S., Miller, W.R., Corner, S. and Kahlich, L., *Intercessory prayer in the treatment of alcohol abuse and dependence: a pilot investigation.* Alternative Therapies in Health and Medicine 3 (6): 79-86, 1997.

Webster's College Dictionary, Random House Kernerman, K Dictionaries Ltd, 2010.

About the Author

With a background in Psychology – MAs in Clinical Psychology and Social Psychology from Paris Sorbonne, Yveline spent 20 years in humanitarian work.

She trained as a Life Coach (Results Coaching School) and an NLP Master Practitioner (Strong NLP), then in Addiction Therapy, graduating with an MSc in Addiction Psychology and Counselling from London South Bank University.

She worked as an addiction therapist for the UK Charity *Street Walk* with trafficked women.

Then she facilitated groups for the Detox Centre *Equinox*, creating a programme of meetings for detoxing clients based on the SMART recovery programme (Self-Management And Recovery Training). There, she trained nurses in group facilitating.

At HAB (Homeless Action in Barnet, London, UK), she worked as a volunteer addiction counsellor.

She now has a small private counselling clientele in London.